Boxing's, Greatest Interviews!!

Boxing Biggest Star's Speak! Ray Leonard to Oscar De La Hoya to Sylvester Stallone!

By
Richard Scurti

iUniverse, Inc.
New York   Bloomington

Boxing's, Greatest Interviews!!
Boxing Biggest Star's Speak! Ray Leonard to Oscar De La Hoya to Sylvester Stallone!

Copyright © 2008 by Richard Scurti

All rights reserved. No part of this book may be used or reproduced by any means, graphic, electronic, or mechanical, including photocopying, recording, taping or by any information storage retrieval system without the written permission of the publisher except in the case of brief quotations embodied in critical articles and reviews.

The views expressed in this work are solely those of the author and do not necessarily reflect the views of the publisher, and the publisher hereby disclaims any responsibility for them.
iUniverse books may be ordered through booksellers or by contacting:

iUniverse
1663 Liberty Drive
Bloomington, IN 47403
www.iuniverse.com
1-800-Authors (1-800-288-4677)

Because of the dynamic nature of the Internet, any Web addresses or links contained in this book may have changed since publication and may no longer be valid. The views expressed in this work are solely those of the author and do not necessarily reflect the views of the publisher, and the publisher hereby disclaims any responsibility for them.

ISBN: 978-0-595-47947-4 (pbk)

Printed in the United States of America

I don't know if these really truly are the greatest boxing interviews… but I like to think so, at least, I like to think that they are. These aren't just stories or interviews…they're glimpses into the lives of professional fighters, some of whom are living, while a few of the others are already dead. This book isn't just about that though, if you like writing and have always wondered about how to break into the business of being a professionally paid writer, than believe it or not, this is also the book for you. Because this book, tells a little bit of my own story, as well as the fighters and more importantly, how I got the interviews. I've included a post and pre-fight wrap up for people to read a bit about what it actually took to get these interviews with boxing's biggest and greatest stars, everyone is here, from Sugar Ray Leonard to Oscar De La Hoya to even film stars like, Sylvester Stallone. I hope that this book is enjoyable for everyone to read and more importantly, I hope that maybe these interviews will help to inspire some people to continue on in life, the same way that the boxing interviews that I read growing up had inspired me. I have nearly twenty of the biggest names in boxing and the world of boxing entertainment listed below, I hope that you, the reader enjoy reading them, as much as I did in getting them and then getting them published…here are the results.

DEDICATIONS

"This book is dedicated to God, the Father, who without whom, all things in this world mean nothing and to my unborn child, Jaedyn Scurti...who died on September 13th 2007...may God unite us both again, Jaedyn". To my family, my Mom and Dad (my father is my first and only true hero in this world and Dad, without your help and interest in boxing...this book could not have been written at all) my wife Alicia, who's been a giant help and who without her help every step of the way, this book wouldn't have been written and my brother Chris who's put up with everything from childhood...sorry about that, Bro!" my Nanny and Pop-Pop Brown, Nanny and Pop-Pop Scurti, my great aunts and uncles, who've been putting up with me from day one...(not everything was all my fault...just partially my fault) my best friend, Laszlo Pokorny and Lisa Reif, thanks for all the great words of encouragement and excellence. Mike Acri, world famous promoter for even getting me started by giving me the chance to talk to you in Canostata, NY and for letting me interview Paul...Thanks, Mike! Thanks to both of my editors as well; to both Greg Juckett and Sean Sullivan at Boxing Digest Magazine. Lastly, but most importantly, I really want to say thank you to all of my family and friends for being the incredible support unit, who've all been there for me from day one...I've been very lucky to have been born into such an incredible family and with such phenomenal friends...thank you everyone!

CONTENTS

AARON PRYOR INTERVIEW	1
PAUL SPADAFORA INTERVIEW	13
MICKY WARD INTERVIEW	23
"PAULIE MALIGNAGGI" INTERVIEW	29
"LOU DIBELLA" INTERVIEW	31
KOSTYA TSYZU INTERVIEW	35
RICKY HATTON INTERVIEW	55
BERNARD HOPKINS INTERVIEW	63
OSCAR DE LA HOYA INTERVIEW	69
CHRISTY MARTIN INTERVIEW	77
DIEGO CORRALES INTERVIEW!	83
O'NEIL BELL INTERVIEW!	89
"SUGAR" RAY LEONARD INTERVIEW	97
BUDDY MCGIRT INTERVIEW	117
KEN BUCHANAN INTERVIEW	125
SYLVESTER STALLONE INTERVIEW	131

AARON PRYOR INTERVIEW PRE-FIGHT:

Aaron Pryor was easy...not easy as in the great uncrowned champion that Pryor was all during the early eighties, but easy as in, how I got the interview! After contacting Boxing Digest and getting my first story on the five-greatest fighters of all-time published within their pages, I knew that I had to get them another story, preferably an interview. At the time, I didn't have the knowledge or the contacts to interview an Oscar De La Hoya or a Sugar Ray Leonard, but I did know from going up to the Boxing Hall of Fame in Canastota last year with my Dad that, up there, were tons of *former* fighters who were very, big but, in *their time* and more importantly...they were all accessible to me. Every time I would go up to the hall of fame in Canastota former champions would be sitting there in the casino and hotels which surround Canastota during hall of fame weekend and were always more than happy to either talk or sign autographs with their fans. The biggest problem for me was...which boxer would get the immediate attention of Boxing Digest's editor, Greg Juckett? I finally settled on Aaron Pryor. Why? Mostly for a couple of very big reasons; Pryor was to me, a very big hero of mine growing up. I always felt like I was always the very best at almost anything I ever touched or concentrated on intently and because of that, a lot of times, people in positions of power would see that, get scared and any positions for growth or advancement...were quickly closed off to me. With Aaron Pryor, you had fighter who early in his career, had nothing but doors closed on him too, because of how talented he was. He was, "too good for his own good" as the old saying in boxing goes and that was something that I could definitely identify with, upon leaving high school and entering the crappiness of the work world in a small town. So, a lot of times when I'd come home from a work interview that I didn't get and become a little depressed because I was refused some advancement, I'd put a video my Dad had of Aaron Pryor on in the vcr and become

1

motivated by his performances inside the boxing ring. Aaron Pryor, in case you don't know much about him, was an uncrowned champion in the light weight division during the early 1980's. But, before that, Pryor had fought as an amateur before the 1976 Olympics alongside of such luminaries as; Michael and Leon Spinks, Howard Davis jr. and "Sugar" Ray Leonard. In 1975, he lost a controversial split decision to Howard Davis jr. a fight that many people who were there, felt that Pryor had won, but because Pryor was too "streety" and not the "pretty boy" that Davis or "Sugar" Ray Leonard was, he was denied his chance to fight at the Olympics that year, in Montreal, 1976. Davis would go on to win an Olympic gold medal that year and received $200,000 dollars for his first professional fight, along with national television exposure of the event (it was broadcast nationally on NBC during the primetime afternoon slot). Pryor meanwhile, upon turning pro, received $400.00 dollars in *his* first professional fight…against a former kick boxer in Cincinnati, Ohio. Pryor, embittered over the loss to Davis in the amateurs, began to rip his way through the entire lightweight division upon turning pro. He fought like a man possessed and indeed he was now, driven by the demons of poverty alongside of the controversial loss to Davis in the amateurs…he made every lightweight who would fight him pay for it. Pryor kept coming at them, throwing hundreds of hard punches round after round, never tiring and the most incredible thing about him was to me, every time that Pryor got hit right on the chin and he hit the floor…he would jump right back up again and attack! Needless to say, Aaron Pryor' fights really helped inspire me to continue on days when, I would have probably just given up and gone home. Pryor eventually rose up in the rankings as a lightweight and encountered the kind of door closing to his talent, because he was so good, none of the lightweight champions at the time would risk a fight with him and so he languished there for a while. Finally, he was given a chance to for the jr. welterweight championship (Pryor had to jump up an entire weight class in order to even get a chance to fight for a title, as no lightweight champion would fight him) against Antonio Cervantes, a champion who had made over six defenses of his title and highly respected. Pryor knocked him out within six rounds and he had his championship. But the demons that drove him to such spectacular heights…could not be quenched and upon defeating hall of famer, Alexis Arguello twice, he succumbed to the demons of cocaine and crack, before abdicating his throne. I looked at what had happened to Aaron Pryor and I gulped and took a deep breath, I decided that I wouldn't be driven by my desires ever... no matter how hard that struggle was for me. I interviewed Pryor because of this and the fact that Pryor was a "fight fans fighter", a guy that the everyday fight fan could identify with and talked about and hence'...would read about. But mostly, I interviewed him *because he was accessible*, I met with him and his wife Frankie at the 2001 HOF and he was so impressed with my knowledge of boxing and his career in particular, that he had given me his business card with his e-mail and phone number on it. They seemed nice and I e-mailed his wife (I was too shy and scared at the time to actually try and call them!), Frankie Pryor and she said to send a list of questions by e-mail to them and she'll make that Aaron answered them. "Yeah, right" I thought, "He isn't going to answer" I figured he'd be just like all the others...lip service. But lo and behold' an e-mail came back with all the answers to my questions already typed in by Frankie herself! Now, I had my very first interview done for Boxing Digest magazine! I was ecstatic! And I realized a very important lesson when dealing or negotiating with people...*YOU MUST HAVE SOMETHING TO OFFER THEM...ALWAYS!* Wish I'd known that sooner, but anyway, below is the original transcript of the interview that I had done with Aaron "The Hawk" Pryor...I hope you like it.

EXCLUSIVE INTERVIEW WITH AARON "THE HAWK" PRYOR!!!

By
Richard Scurti

1. Aaron, what exactly got you interested in the sport of boxing?

I had always been very athletic as a kid. I enjoyed a lot of sports including baseball, football, and basketball. However, I was just too small to be any good. Although there was a boxing gym in my neighborhood, I had never been there. One day when I was 13 I got into a fight with a guy who was much bigger than me. The coach of the boxing gym came outside to break up the fight. He suggested that I should be boxing inside of a gym inside of street fighting outside. I went inside that day and just never left!

2. What was it like growing up in the mean streets of Cincinnati, Ohio?

What do you think it was like? It wasn't the best, but it also wasn't the worst. When you grow up in an environment where there are a lot of problems at home, you learn quickly to depend only on yourself. Maybe that's why I was so good at boxing. I knew I could count on me. I had been doing that for a long time. As kids, all my brothers and sisters struggled for food and shelter. That's why I like speaking at inner-city schools and sharing my story with kids who are struggling today. You have to learn to move beyond your past.

3. It must have been very frustrating knowing that you were without a doubt the best lightweight in the world, and yet no lightweight in the world, champion or otherwise, would try and fight you. Any idea why?

I think that HBO explained this very well in their Legendary Nights Series. In the Tale of Pryor-Arguello, they made mention that I was a very dangerous fighter and without a big money fight in my past, most fighters in my weight class didn't want to take the chance of getting beat for a smaller payday. I have to agree that it was those two factors: getting beat and the small purse.

4. Did you ever spar with Ray Mancini, Tommy Hearns, or Ray Leonard in the amateurs or anywhere else? How close were you to getting a shot at any of the lightweight champs in the 1980's?

I was defending my '75 National Amateur Jr. Welterweight title when I fought Tommy Hearns in the National Golden Glove Finals in the Orange Bowl in Miami, Florida in 1976. This is the same place I would beat Arguello just 6 years later. Anyway, I beat Tommy which disqualified him for the Olympics. That was back in the days when amateurs fought without headgear and there was not the safety rules in place that we have today for our young men. It was more like a pro fight. That footage is still floating around. You can definitely see both of our pro styles already in place. Ray Leonard and I have been friends since our amateur days. We go back a long way. I used to stay with Ray and his family for months at a time in Maryland when we were both first starting out. I was hired as Ray's sparring partner, after the Olympics. We both had a natural ability for boxing and with that comes the competition. I really believe that our past friendship may have hindered our fighting as pros. While Ray Mancini and I also go back to our amateur days, I never had the chance to work with him.

That would have been great. Most fans don't realize that so many of us who were champs in the 1980's have friendships with each other than go back to our amateur days when we were teenagers. Holmes, Spinks brothers, Leonard, Hearns, Hagler, Pryor, just to name a few. We were all in negotiations together throughout the whole time I boxed. Timing just wasn't right.

5. Any truth to the rumor that you had floored "Sugar" Ray Leonard in sparring and that some people who watched you spar at that time felt that you might have had Leonard's "number"?

Yes, I did knock Ray down in sparring. That's how I lost my job with him! Ha! Ha! That's the great debate in boxing history. Who would have won the fight between Ray and me? Just as the fans have their opinion on that fight, so do Ray and I.

6. In all honesty, how would Aaron Pryor at his all-time best, do against the all-time best of: Sugar "Ray" Leonard, Roberto Duran, and Tommy Hearns? How close were you to a match-up with the great Roberto Duran?

When people talk boxing, they talk about a fighter's heart. What is he made of? You don't get to the top of your game and become a champ, unless you truly believe that you can beat them all. There's no way you can go up against a guy in the ring if you think there's a chance you can lose. Ray and I sparred and I can honestly say that we would have given each other a hell of a fight. As for Hearns, I beat him a year before we turned pros. Duran? I could have won that fight, but it was never going to happen. Panama Lewis, my trainer, had close family ties to Duran and that prevented the fight from happening.

7. Who hit you the hardest? In the amateurs and as a pro? How hard did Tommy Hearns hit you when you beat him as an amateur in the 1970's, was he a single shot guy even back then? And most importantly who did you hit the hardest with a single shot?

Yes, Tommy was a hard hitter but in the amateurs I give all credit to a guy named Norman Goins for having the hardest single shot. He hit me with a body shot and I thought he had killed me. Fortunately, they had a good ref during that fight who jumped in and gave me my first ever stoppage. Only had one in my career. Without a doubt, the hardest hitting guy I ever came up against in the pros was a guy named Dujuan Johnson. We fought in Cleveland on November 14, 1981 for the WBA jr. welterweight championship. It was a TKO in the 7th round, but what a 7 rounds it was. That guy had power. Interestingly enough, he was trained by Emmanuel Steward and had Tommy Hearns in his corner. I think that they were trying to get revenge for the fight I had with Tommy in the amateurs, but it didn't happen. As for my hardest hit I ever gave, I would have to say it was the over-hand right I caught Alexis Arguello with in the 14th round during our first fight. It was that shot that won the fight for me. In fact, I believe that was the best punch of my career.

8. Aaron, you were a physical fighting, marvel fighting all fifteen rounds if need be without even tiring. How did Aaron Pryor train for his fights in terms of roadwork or weights to achieve that kind of stamina?

My amateur coach got me on a routine that I basically stayed with through my whole pro career. Training is everything. Natural ability is second. I believe the most important thing in training is running. Run, run, and run. I ran 5 miles a day, 5 days a week. We got up early in the morning to run and then back home to take it easy until the afternoon workout session. I never used weights and don't believe in them today for my fighters. I would start my work-out with conditioning exercises, hit the heavy bag until it wasn't heavy anymore, speed bag, spar, and then more conditioning exercises. Of course, diet was critical. That was my routine 5 days a week, each and every week from the time I was 13 until the day I retired. Consistency is the key. When it came time for a fight, we just stepped up the pace. I would train as if I was going to fight 40 or 50 rounds, so 15 rounds seemed like nothing. That is where the stamina came from. Today I just run and it's amazing how much stamina and conditioning you get from just running on a regular, consistent basis.

8. What is your relationship to Tim Austin after he was knocked out in his last fight?

Timmy and I have been friends since he was just a kid, and we are very close. I really regret that I wasn't in his corner this last fight. The Cincinnati boxing community is very, very, close and has a rich history. You go to our gyms here and you will see Cincinnati champions of yesterday on the wall; Ezzard Charles, Wallace Bud Smith, Tony Tubbs, Freddie Miller and Aaron Pryor. Then you will see the champions of today and tomorrow in the ring. On any given day, you can find Tim Austin, Ricardo Williams, Ravae Springs, Dale Crowe and a host of other fighters in all various stages of their workout. As for Timmy, I have been to training camp with him and worked his corner for three of his title fights. We work together here in Cincinnati in the gym also. I just saw him the other night and he is doing good, planning to move up in weight. I think he should have moved up a long time ago. Timmy has tremendous talent and you can expect even greater things from my friend in the future.

9. Seeing the immediate results and success that Buddy McGirt has had as a trainer, shouldn't other young up and coming fighters seek out former jr. welterweight champion Aaron Pryor to train them? Any

young fighters you are bringing up or is their any established fighter that you would like to work with?

I am very happy for Buddy's success. He really enjoys his work. I have been approached by a lot of young fighters wanting me to train them. I have to be honest here and let you know that unless you are willing to take boxing as serious as I did, I'm not interested. You have to give it 100%, or you will get nothing out of it. I have tried working with fighters who are up and coming, but I feel that my style of coaching is better suited to fighters who are near, or already at the top of their game. That's what I love about working with Tim Austin. He is a pro and a joy to work with. I do work with my sons, who are young in their careers, but they are family! Stephan is 8-0 as a pro and Aaron, Jr. is coming along just fine in the amateurs.

10. What does Aaron Pryor do for fun and work now that you are retired? I understand that you run your own website www.hawktime.com and it looks like a good place for your fans and young fighters who need guidance to get in touch with you? Your thoughts or comments?

I am currently celebrating 10 years cocaine-free and life has never been better. I travel all over the country for personal appearances, speaking engagements, and autograph signing sessions. Church and family are my full-time job today. I have been a Deacon at New Friendship Baptist Church for 8 years now. As for my family, we have a lot of excitement going on. I just became a grandfather. Aaron Pryor III was born last month. Not only did we just celebrate his birth, but we are preparing for a wedding. My
long-time fiancée' of 12 years, Frankie Wagner-Pryor, who is well known within the boxing community, will become my wife on June 5th at the International Boxing Hall of Fame during Induction Weekend. She has been by my side through all the good and bad times and we are thrilled to have this ceremony at our second home. We would love

Richard Scurti

for all our fans to check out our website, at www.hawktime.com. There are photos and information on my career. We also have a memorabilia shop on the site where you can purchase autographed photos, boxing gloves and lithographs. I love hearing from my fans, so please stop by and visit.

You can get in touch with Aaron "The Hawk" Pryor at his Official Website: www.hawktime.com in regards to career info, speaking engagements, and memorabilia from the former all-time great Champion Aaron Pryor!!

POST FIGHT:

In retrospect now, I was very thrilled to have this opportunity to have interviewed a hero of mine like, Aaron Pryor! My first interview in print, I was so excited! Even if it was done by e-mail and he had been retired for years…I was still, very excited to have received Frankie's e-mail and then have Boxing Digest put it in print, more than I originally thought at the time. Since this interview, I got to talk with Ray Leonard about the Pryor sparring sessions (you'll just have to read into it later on in this book, well' you didn't think I reveal if Pryor put Ray down for good this early in the book did you? ha! ha!) and he was also very candid about their friendship with each other. All in all, it was a very, very, big moment for me both as the beginnings of becoming a pro writer and as a person. After this, I decided to help out my old buddy, Mike Acri, who had got me, started in the boxing business to begin with and I made arrangements to interview his current fighter, lightweight champion of the world, Paul Spadafora.

PAUL SPADAFORA INTERVIEW PRE-FIGHT:

Paul was the first. The first *real* boxing interview that I did for Boxing Digest with an active fighter and who was also a current champion in the lightweight division. I had written a couple of other stories for Boxing Digest before, a two part story on the five greatest fighters of all time and of course, the interview I had done by e-mail with Aaron Pryor and his wife, Frankie. At the time, I had *no money*! I'm not kidding! I was working at a job that I didn't really like and spent the bulk of my time, drinking in the bars of my area and smoking afterwards, hoping to meet someone special after boozing it up all night. So when I got this call from Mike Acri, Spadafora' promoter, at ten o'clock at night, (I was half asleep, but I *had* asked him to call me back earlier in the day) where I was given this chance to drive out to Pittsburgh some 350 miles away (I'm not sure if that's the right amount of miles...it may as well have been 1,500 miles to me at the time) I jumped at the chance...without thinking. The truth was, I had about a hundred dollars in the bank at the time and my car was running badly (it was border line overheating almost all the time) but hey, I told myself, "how often do you get the opportunity to go out and interview the lightweight champion of the world"! So I grabbed eighty dollars out of the bank (for gas) and took off for Pittsburgh. It took me eight hours to get there (it usually takes about five to six hours) but, I finally got there and pulled into my hotel. After getting changed and talking with Mike, I was told to go downstairs to meet up with Paul. I think up until then, the seriousness of what I was and what I was doing hadn't quite hit me yet...I was still in dreamland after driving through the wilds and half the state of Pennsylvania! I went downstairs nervous and sat in the lobby, my back pressed against the wall and waited to meet with Paul Spadafora, lightweight champion of the world. After sitting there for about fifteen minutes within the hotel lobby, the revolving door spun around and in walked the lightweight champion of the world, Paul Spadafora. I had only seen him on TV before and it was a really very, surreal, but' exciting, experience. "Are you Scurti…the writer…for the boxing magazine?" asked Paul as he looked down at me, with his shaven head and tattooed laden fingers that read, "Love" and "Hate" across the backs of each of his knuckles. I've come to accept one of the many things my dad had taught me growing up as fact, one of which was that, real fighters have a certain *look* to them. Whenever you first meet them, a mixture of no fear and no surprises' is in their faces' every time that you meet them, that'll just let you know…right off the bat…you know they're seen some shit… and well' *Paul had that look.*

We left in an old beat up car along with his conditioning coach, Chef and we drove around for about an hour within the Pittsburg ghetto, before arriving at Paul's house. We were going to see his home first before going out to eat at his favorite Italian restaurant, the best place in Pittsburgh. When we arrived at his home, I started my first real interview. *Man was I nervous!* I remember all during the time I sat in the car with Paul, I wasn't nervous at all, but once when I arrived at the house with a group of people watching, I began to sweat. The interview was very good, I sat next to him in Paul's house and he began to get cranky as the interview progressed. Finally, after about a half an hour (I had no idea at the time of how long an interview was even supposed to last!) I ran out of questions and it seemed like Paul, was about to run out of patience, I finished the interview, thanked everyone for their time and prepared myself for my long six-hour trip back to New Jersey. At the time, I probably would have glowed proudly the whole way back to New Jersey (I had just interviewed current, lightweight champion Paul Spadafora) except, that I was a lot more interested in making sure that my car didn't break down on I-95 on my way back home.

"PAUL SPADAFORA"

BD: Hey Paul, what got you started in boxing?
PS: "Well, my brother Harry was a fighter and my grandfather fought, so you now my whole family fought, it was in the blood to do it. I had a heavy bag in my basement, so I started hitting the heavy bag when I was litter and after that I just wanted to be able to go to the gym like my brother and just fight."

BD: When did you first start going to the gym to actually learn how to fight? How young were you?
PS: "I first started going down to my trainer PK's gym when I was like fourteen, he started showing me how to do…you know, the basic stuff."

BD: Did you fight amateur?
PS: "I had eighty-five amateur fights, I won the Golden Gloves a couple times, State Champion a couple times, Ohio State fair Champion three times. I wasn't a great amateur, but, I was pretty good, you know?"

BD: Did you get into a lot of fights as a kid, growing up on the street?
PS: "No, I didn't get into a whole lot of fights on the street…ever since I started boxing…it kind of pulled me away from all that."

BD: Do you feel that it might have kept you out of trouble a lot more, since you discovered boxing so young?
PS: "yeah…definitely."

BD: Was there any fighters you looked up to?
PS: "My favorite fighter was Tommy Hearns."

BD: What did you like most about Hearns?

PS: "I liked his attitude, you know, when he got hurt...He'd come back...He had a very big, strong, heart."

BD: Who would you say that you most modeled yourself after in terms of your own boxing style?
PS: "I think a little bit of Pernell Whitaker and James Toney, too."

BD: How do you feel about comparisons made between you and another Pittsburgh boxing legend, Billy Conn?
PS: "I never rally saw too many of Billy Conn's fights, I watched a tape of him fighting Joe Louis and he seemed like he was a pretty good boxer, but not really a great boxer."

BD: You're the first champion to come out of Pittsburgh in like, sixty years! It must feel pretty good?
PS: (Paul smiles sheepishly with his hand on his head, suddenly shy and embarrassed): "Yeah...Yeah, it does! (Laughing to himself good-naturedly)

BD: Is there a move up to junior-welterweight in your immediate future?
PS: "I'd like to fight the rematch with Leonard Dorin next! Then maybe get a chance to fight against Arturo Gatti."

BD: Do you think you'd have a good chance at beating Gatti?
PS: "Yeah, I think I do...I think styles make fights, I think, maybe I got a great chance of bust'in him up!"

BD: So, you have trouble making the lightweight limit now?
PS: "It was too hard...It took the love out of it, you know? I'm fighting two fights...I'm fighting me and I'm fighting to make weight."

BD: So what do you think you'll do differently in the second fight with Dorin?

PS: " I think I'll be more accurate, I'll be boxing more, use my jab a lot more, I mean' it's going to' be the same thing, I'm going to' fight the same, slipping inside...I'm a better inside fighter than he is."

BD: How about a match-up with Kostya Suzy for any of the jr. welterweight titles?
PS: "I mean, that's the ultimate goal, you know what I mean? Try to become the 140 pound world champion."

BD: You feel you'll be stronger at jr. welterweight?
PS: "I'll be a lot stronger...a lot more energy and everything."

BD: Is there any stories from growing up that you want to talk about, that made you grow as a fighter?
PS: I think, when I started boxing and I kind of grew up to a whole other level, was when I fought in the ABF regional championships, with my brother Harry, who was number three in the country. We were training with my grandfather and we went down to D.C. and...I lost...and that just...hurt so bad, because I dedicated everything to boxing...I quit school and everything...just to be a boxer. I went into the Golden Gloves after that and just...you know, tore it up."

BD: Tell me a little bit about your background, how you grew up?
PS: "Where I grew up, I mean'...it was very real life, you know? I grew up with my mom. My mom raised us, all three of my brothers. We all played sports, with my brother Harry and me, be' in a fighter."

BD: You grew up Italian?
PS: "Yeah' my Dad's from Italy and I'm also part Calabrese. We didn't really have a lot of money growing up...we used to rent our old house for $200.000 a month...and when I first started boxing...I used to jog up the hill around my neighborhood about five miles, every day."

BD: That must have given you a lot more of a desire to...?
PS: "It did...it definitely did. I think all fighters have to know what it's like to struggle for a while. It brings the toughness in the heart out of you."

BD: Would you ever consider moving up to welterweight?
PS: "I'll probably retire at that weight, 147 pounds."

BD: How about a big fight against any of the welterweight champs?
PS: "Man...definitely...I would hope so you know? But, I want to see how long I stay at 140 pounds for now."

BD: What was your proudest boxing moment?
PS: "When I fought Victoriano Sosa...I was knocked out on my feet and I had to struggle to get through the fight...I watch it every now and again...see how much heart I got."

BD: What was your toughest fight?
PS: "Definitely Sosa."

BD: Who do you think you hit the hardest?
PS: "I think I hit Leonard Dorin pretty hard. I was really sit-in down on my punches and I hit him hard to the body and Pito Cardona, too."

BD: Who do you think hit you the hardest?
PS: "Sosa, he's a very hard puncher. Sosa's probably the hardest puncher in the lightweight division."

BD: Any personal goals you have?
PS: "To be the 140 pound champion, fight Kostya Tsyzu and unify all the titles, and after boxing, try to use my brains and keep my money for security."

BD: would you ever consider being a trainer?
PS: "No, not really."

BD: Will you always be a part of Pittsburgh?
PS: "Definitely!"

BD: Who do you think, is the most talented fighter that you like, fighting today?
PS: "James Toney, he's a very good fighter. But the most talented fighter, has got to be Roy Jones...a natural."

BD: Out of all the people that you sparred with...who was the toughest?
PS: "Lamar Murphy, definitely, my toughest. He's the only guy...I mean; I can't believe that he isn't a world champion."

BD: What went through your mind, when you won the world lightweight championship?
PS: "I couldn't believe it...I was in shock...I did what I'd always wanted to do...become champion of the world...it was like a dream come true. That was the best moment of my life...it made it all... worth it."

BD: How do you train?
PS: "Eat, sleep, drink right, live right."

BD: Rumor has it that you had hurt and put Floyd Mayweather jr. through the ropes during a sparring session in 1999, your comments?
PS: "It wasn't anything serious, you know what, I mean? I thought I got the better of him, but he wasn't in the gym all that long...I would love to fight him."

BD: Dorin, Mayweather, Gatti, who would you like to fight first?
PS: "Mayweather, that'd be a dream come true, then I'd like Dorin and Gatti, next."

BD: How many tattoos do you have on your body and will you get any more?
PS: "Seven tattoos and a whole lot more."

BD: Anything you want to say to your fans?
PS: "Look forward to me as the next 140 pound champion."

POST FIGHT:

I got home at 3:45 in the morning and immediately conked out. The next couple days were a blur for me, a mixture of mostly work and family stuff and I just felt swamped by everything else I was doing between work and family and school, besides trying to write for Boxing Digest magazine. I hadn't even gotten the interview done yet, when I got a call from Boxing Digest editor, Greg Juckett and he asked if I had done the interview yet. "Of course' I said "I was just getting ready to send it all over to you, but I'm on my cell phone at work." He asked if "I could wait a couple of days before sending it in and that, given the circumstances, he might be able to get it into the next issue"... maybe. Sweat immediately began to break out on my forehead and I saw all of my, new, professional, writing career... go immediately out the window!

"I can send it over to you immediately as soon I get home" I said, half pleading and also half hoping that this wouldn't be my only shot at the big time. I could just see it now... I was effectively finished before I ever, even got started! Life suddenly seemed like it was still, all the same, never getting the opportunity, when I was able to do something. "I don't think you understand...have you read the papers, lately?" said Greg, "it's all over the news. "What is?" I said, I had to confess that now, I was a little bit curious as to why the current, undisputed, lightweight champion of the world, wasn't going directly into the pages of Boxing Digest magazine. "Haven't you heard, it's all over the news and everything...Paul Spadafora shot his girlfriend in the front chest...she's in the hospital... in critical condition...I don't know for certain, said Greg, "but she's pretty bad off."

I was stunned, I couldn't believe it! Greg asked me to I write something up as a potential disclaimer' just in case he was found guilty of the crime. I said, "okay" and hung up the phone with Greg and just, stared off into space. I couldn't believe it... Paul Spadafora had shot his girlfriend and he had been arrested and charged with the crime

(Paul would eventually do some time for the shooting and his girlfriend would get back with him and have a baby together, I also, did the very first interview with Paul upon his release from prison in 2006)... and...I... Richard Scurti...had the last, official, interview with him! Little did I know... that this was just a precursor of things, which were yet to come. After all that, I would then go and interview a fighter who fought in possibly the greatest, three-fight trilogy ever within the jr. welterweight division, out of the two...I got to interview one of them...Micky Ward.

MICKY WARD INTERVIEW PRE-FIGHT:

After the Paul Spadafora interview was printed in the February, 2004 issue of Boxing Digest, I knew that I had to give them another one... quickly. If I was going to keep any type of momentum going and I was going to make my name known...at least in the boxing world. All during this time, the jr. welterweight division was really heating up, the division was becoming stocked with great fights and fighters like Kostya Tsyzu, Micky Ward, Paul Spadafora, Sharmba Mitchell, Zab Judah...made sure that every fight was a potential barnburner. Out of all these guys, two of them, gave the world of boxing an epic three-fight encounter; Arturo Gatti and Micky Ward. I had been a fan of both of these guys since the mid-1990's and had seen most of Arturo Gatti's great fights in Atlantic City. So you can imagine the interest I had in interviewing Micky Ward, (who had just retired after the three brutal wars with Arturo Gatti) when I asked our editor Greg Juckett, about doing a piece on Ward for the magazine. Once again, I have to thank Greg Juckett, for his incredible help all during this time, without his great help, almost none of these interviews would've been possible. He gave me the contact for Ward's promoter, Lou Dibella and I gave his office a call and I proposed interviewing Micky Ward alongside of Lou Dibella's fast rising, jr. welterweight star, Paulie Malignaggi... as well as an interview with Lou Dibella himself, for Boxing Digest magazine. Lou is the kind of guy who's very smart, graduated from Harvard and literally, has an IQ of around 200 somewhere...you can actually hear the guy stop...*and then think*. "No" said Lou pausing and immediately my heart sank, "but, I'll tell you what you can do...you can talk to them both, profiling the differences between both Micky and Paulie, with me as the intermediary, just call my receptionist back and he'll give you the numbers." (Basically paraphrasing everything that I had just said, but I guess, just in his own words, "okay, whatever makes him happy", I figured) My heart jumped up into my throat, "thank you so much for your time Lou, I really appreciate this I'll

Richard Scurti

call—" -click- that was it! The guy just hung up on me, midstream and mid talk! But, hey' I figured, that was okay, as long as I got my interviews with them and especially Micky Ward…I'd be more than happy. Naturally, after I called back and got the date and the times set up, they gave me- Malignaggi first, Micky Ward second and Lou Dibella last. Interestingly enough for me, I did the interview with Micky Ward on my birthday, February 10th 2004, on the phone, in the group home I worked at in Ringoes, NJ, right in the middle of the afternoon…I'll never forget it. Anyway, here's all three interviews, just as they appeared within the pages of Boxing Digest magazine!

"MICKEY WARD"
INTERVIEW

BD: How's retirement treating you, Mick?

MW: "It's going good, you know, can't complain, been keeping busy. I've been training a few fighters up her for the amateurs and stuff in Lowell, MA...Shawn Ecklund my nephew, a couple of young guys... Frazier, Mattryland...who's another good fighter from South Boston. So yeah I'm keeping busy."

BD: How'd you get started in boxing?

MW: "Well, I was about seven years old and my brother Dickie (Dickie Ecklund) was training me then, teaching me how to hit the heavy bag on my hands and knees. I didn't really have any knowledge or interest in the game then...you know, being so young...I used to just go in there and try to take their heads off."

BD: Did you fight amateur?

MW: Yeah, you know, I fought amateur won a couple of silver, golden gloves titles, which opened more doors...the ABF nationals, CGI regionals, you know, stuff like that. I'll actually be the assistant coach for the New England Amateur tournament in April or May of this year and then we'll be going to England to compete, so I'm excited by all that."

BD: How old were you when you turned pro?

MW: "I was nineteen years old when I turned pro and I fought like every few months. Even before that, I was never really into boxing at all during high school. Dickie was into boxing, but I was more into other sports like baseball and wrestling and I played baseball and ran cross country as a freshman in high school."

BD: Did you get into a lot of fights as a kid?

MW: "No, not a lot. I grew up in the Acree-Lowell, MA area and then moved to the Highlands, I mean, there was a lot of trouble around, but it wasn't my thing. I mean, between the ages of sixteen to nineteen I had a few street fights, but I just got along with everyone mostly…It's not my thing to have a problem with anyone…black, Spanish, white… everyone's the same to me."

BD: Did the fights with Arturo Gatti take a lot out of you? Personally or physically? Which of those three fights would you say was your toughest?

MW: "Fights…they were more like wars (laughs)! I guess they were all like equally tough, you know…but probably the second fight in Atlantic City, I don't know how I made it, but he caught me on the ear and floored me and I was like Ow! You bastard! (laughs) And after that last fight too, my eyesight was a little bad so that was a tough one too…but you would have to talk to Arturo about that!" (laughs)

BD: Speaking of that left hook, how did you perfect that? Was it something you always had or did you just develop it?

MW: "It sounds odd, but it's like one day I just woke up with it. I did have to practice using it though, after I had the bone from my pelvis put into my right had…I had to use the left more. Before that, my right was my stronger punch."

BD: Tell us how you used to train both then and now.

MW: "I used to run like maybe three, four miles a day, now I do interval training on the treadmill walk, track, hills, not always at one time though. I'll be running in the Boston Marathon this year…I must be crazy. (laughs) But it's good you know…I'll be running for kids with disabilities so that's good too!"

BD: What will you be doing now that you're officially retired?

MW: "Do whatever, I own a tanning salon with my fiancée…she runs it…I have my own house…train, go back to paving…you know, just…weigh my options."

BD: When did you first get hooked up with promoter, Lou DiBella and what do you think of up coming 140-pounder Paul Malignaggi and do you think he can take over your mantle as boxing most exciting 140-pound fighter?

MW: "Lou got me around the time of the Shea Neary or maybe the Antonio Diaz fight, which is also one of my toughest fights. Lou got me Leija, I mean Lou's excellent! I mean, he had faith in me, he made me money and I got to keep it. People like Lou, my manager Sal Lonano, the guys from HBO; I can't say enough good things about them. Just only good things. "Paulie can fight! You know he'll eventually have to step it up to see what he really has…all the speed and the tools, to use. He'll have to grow and fight more, but for him…the sky's the limit. I give him credit…he has the tools and he knows what to do. He has it all…it's up to him now."

BD: How come there was never a match-up between you and 140-pound champion Kostya Tsyzu?

MW: "Well, I guess you know, I never really rose that high enough and …I had no title or anything. I just kind of knew it would never happen…one is Showtime against HBO…with no title or real ranking…I guess it was just everything…that's why that fight never came off."

BD: Before we go, is there anything you want to say to you many fight fans out there, who read Boxing Digest?

MW: "Yes, I want to thank everyone who stood behind me and had faith in me and never gave up on me. I wish Arturo Gatti the best…thirty rounds…that was a lot! And I just want to say thanks to everyone who believed in me every step of the way."

"PAULIE MALIGNAGGI" INTERVIEW

BD: What got you started in boxing?

PM: "I started boxing when I was sixteen, got into trouble in school, got thrown out of school, started living with my grandparents and I had an uncle who went to Gleason's Gym. This is when I had my first amateur fight, the national title, 2001 U.S. championships at 132 pounds."

BD: When did you first turn pro?

PM: "I didn't really have a lot of the amateur experience at twenty years old, which like some of these other guys have had like Jesse James Leija, or Hector Camacho Jr., but by now at twenty three years old, I'm picking up."

BD: Who were some of your favorite fighters growing up? And was there anybody in particular that you really kind of modeled yourself after?

PM: "Um, probably...Meldrick Taylor, Leonard, Ali...I got fast hands, so I'm slick like them."

BD: How do you train?

PM: "I go to the gym in the morning, work on my conditioning, just a lot of speed training."

BD: What is your relationship with former 140-pounder Mickey Ward and how do you feel about taking over the mantle as Lou DiBella's hot, new, 140-pound action fighter?

PM: "Mickey Ward…he's my man! Man, those wars with Gatti was… man, they were something else! Yeah! But he's a real quiet, humble, guy…you know… not like me! (laughs) But yeah, it's a privilege, and I know that those are some big shoes to fill…I'm looking forward to taking over that mantle!"

BD: Is there anyone in particular that you would like to fight?

PM: "Yes! As a matter of fact there is! Bojado man, me and him had it out face to face and let me tell you something I don't like him! I respect him, but I don't like him…it's a personal thing. So yeah, I'd really like to fight him and settle this once and for all! But, hey I want all those guys out there! I mean Kostya Tsyzu is on the way out anyway."

BD: Is there any type of music that you like to listen to?

PM: "Dance, rock, hip-hop, a little bit of everything."

BD: What do you think of your current relationship with Lou DiBella?

PM: "Lou's a great guy who really had me from day one and he's a super nice, super smart guy, he really looks out for me. I'm hoping I'll keep fighting between 140-147 for Lou, win a couple of titles, like' Whitaker did."

BD: Who did you hit the hardest and what's been your toughest fight so far?

PM: "Bogotá, in the Bogota fight I hit him hard and hurt him bad and my hand was badly injured. I mean, I'm not Tyson, but you could end up on the canvas."

BD: What are you future plans?

PM: "To keep busy, fight the very best out there and win a Jr. Welter weight title in 2004…I'll be the first to do it under DiBella Entertainment."

"LOU DIBELLA" INTERVIEW

BD: Lou, how long have you had Paulie Malignaggi?

LD: "I began with Paulie from the beginning when he was 19 and took him through his first fight and then turned him pro. He's now doing quite well."

BD: Do you see any differences between you two 140-poun protégé's, Mickey Ward and Paul Malignaggi?

LD: "I see Mickey as doing more of his talking in the ring, while, Paulie is more flashy, likes to trash talk both in and out of the ring and carries around a lot of bravado. As far as boxing ability is concerned, Mickey is more or your traditional, come-forward, blue-collar, white, brawler, fighter and Paulie is more of a showman in the ways of a Leonard, or Whitaker, or Ali, fast, flashy hands and stuff. Mickey is quiet whereas Paulie just reacts to things and has a big mouth in and out of the ring."

BD: What do you see in Paulie's immediate future?

PM: "I see Paulie having greater opportunities, Mickey had some great fights, but lost a few and I see Paulie really taking over that mantle and being highly successful. Both men's styles were very different and Paulie really doesn't have that one punch to the liver like Mickey did, but he's a more all-around, complete fighter."

BD: Who do you see next for Paulie as an opponent?

PM: "He'll have to make a step up in a level, to a Ben Tackie, or aim him toward Dimitri Salida."

BD: What do you see next for boxing?

LD: "I say, boxing needs to fight the good fight, it's difficult out there to make money, we need to diversify."

BD: What's next for DiBella Entertainment?

LD: "We might start working with ESPN on another one of its fight series, possibly working with FOX on other stuff. We are also working on a Hi-Def setup with MSG Network, among others. Paulie will most probably be fighting in April; also Mickey has been contacted to sell the rights to his life story. So, there is plenty of stuff in the line up, we're taking it one step at a time."

POST-FIGHT: WRAP-UP

Interestingly enough, I see Micky Ward every year at the boxing hall of fame and he's a genuinely all around nice, good guy…it was a distinct pleasure to have interviewed him. Paulie went on to fight a couple of bigger fights so far and is still a professional. Lou, of course, went on to start a company with hip/hop entrepreneur, Damon Dash (see my other book, "The Boxing/Hip-Hop Connection!" for my interview with Damon Dash, oh' come on now' you didn't really think that I really *wasn't* going to plug my second book in the series within these pages now, did you?) Dash/Dibella entertainment. and actually had a pretty big supporting role in the last (yeah' right) Rocky film, "Rocky Balboa" (more on Sly later on in this book, all right' my big interview with Sly Stallone!) in Dec. 2006. Another big turning point for me, I was proud of my accomplishment and the fact that I got to personally speak with another one of my childhood heroes, when all three of these interviews got printed in the May/June issue of Boxing Digest magazine. But, as great as that was, I felt there were more great interviews out there…that, I just had to get. Micky Ward was a great jr. welterweight, now doubt about it, but the champion of the division, Kostya Tsyzu, was still unaccounted for as an interviewee…I wanted to change all that.

KOSTYA TSYZU INTERVIEW PRE-FIGHT:
"BOLD OF WORD, BOLD OF FIST"

Kostya Tsyzu was a very big interview for me. I had been a huge, fan of Kostya Tsyzu ever since about 94-95, when he first burst upon the international, boxing scene. Tsyzu was an outstanding Russian amateur boxer, who upon turning pro, had compiled a record of 18-0 with 16 ko's before winning the jr. welterweight title by knocking out Jake Rodriguez in 1995. Tsyzu, was a European fighter who *liked to fight* and had explosive fight ending power in either hand… he was one of those rare fighters who seemed destined for greatness. As a young man on his way up, he was a personal hero to me and his fights would actually inspire me to continue when I was down. It was always my dream to fight him as a boxer when I began to train to box in Trenton NJ, in my dreams it would be the American versus the Russian, like in Rocky-six and as usual, in my dreams at least, I would end up winning (in real life I'd have had my head knocked off). So, when I was now, actually writing and looking for my next target to write about, Tsyzu (who had regained the jr. welterweight championship, after being stopped by "cool" Vince Phillips in 1997, and derailing a lucrative, potential match-up with Oscar De La Hoya that year) was the logical choice.

Once again, I called my editor Greg Juckett up and he gave me the contact for a guy named Paul Upham. Paul was a boxing writer who lived in Australia and was a close, personal, friend with both Kostya Tsyzu and the entire Tsyzu camp. I knew that they had recently made a boxing DVD, called "Destiny" which they were trying to promote here in the United States, chronicling Kostya' rise to the championship. Since Tsyzu had won the title again (he would defeat the other two champions Zab Judah and Sharmba Mitchell pretty easily, in the process, he became the first undisputed jr. welterweight champion in over forty years) and was in the process of defending it against Sharmba Mitchell for the second time when I contacted Paul Upham about interviewing Kostya Tsyzu. I picked up my brother Chris' phone and dialed the number that Greg had given me and waited for Paul to answer all the across to the other side of the world, to the Land Down Under, Australia.

It rang and it rang and still…it rang…finally, the phone was picked up and a very sleepy voice croaked out, "hello"? I immediately broke into my sales pitch, "hi this is Richard Scurti from Boxing Digest magazine and I'm calling for Paul Upham". "Speaking" the voice croaked, "I was calling in reference to doing an interview with Kostya Tsyzu." It was silent on the other end for a second, "it's four-thirty in the morning" Paul's voice was barely above a whisper. "Holy shit", I thought, that's early, this guy's going to' be pissed and I'll never get my interview!" I had to give him something big to bite onto, or I'd be sunk. "I'd like to do an interview with Kostya Tsyzu in reference to the "Destiny" DVD he's putting out." It was very quiet on the other end and I gulped, I could feel my chances with this interview, were quickly slipping away. I swallowed hard and uttered, "I'd also like to do interviews with both Kostya' trainer, Johnny Lewis and you on what into the production of the "Destiny" DVD, as well." I wasn't really planning on interviewing both of these guys but, I had to think of something fast and to do interviews with trainers or boxing writers wasn't uncommon to do within the pages of our magazine. "When's your deadline?" "The end of this month", I stammered. I took a deep breath and I heard Paul exhale deeply, it was so late or early in the morning (however you want to look at it), I thought my chances were still sunk. "Let me make some calls first and I'll see what I can do…maybe I can set something up for later on in the week." I let out my breath and exchanged our contacts, before apologizing profusely for waking him up and hung up the phone. I didn't think that much would really come of it to be honest'…I had learned a long time ago to not, "count my chickens before they were ever hatched". I hung up the phone and continued on my drive into Trenton, N.J. that day and drove home afterwards.

About a week went by after my initial phone call to the, "Outback", and I was telling my coworker about everything that had gone on in the, "Land Down Under", when my cell phone rang. It said "unregistered" and being that I had just paid my phone bill, I decided to pick it up, "hello' can I speak to Richard, please?" Said a very familiar voice with the thick Australian accent on the other end, my hands got wet and I was able to croak out, "speaking". "This is Paul Upham, you had called in reference to interviewing Kostya Tsyzu, I've spoken with Kostya's people and they've informed me that they'd be very happy to do the interview with; Kostya Tsyzu, Johnny Lewis and myself. We're looking to do the interview with Kostya on Friday and the others on Sat. and Sunday. In addition, we'd also like to send your own "Destiny" DVD autographed by Kostya as a special memento for you...is Friday night, okay for you to interview, Kostya?"

I was SPEECHLESS!!! My throat went as dry as an empty riverbed and again I was able to croak out , "Not a problem, do you have the number available?" We exchanged times and numbers and I wrote it down with a pen that appeared to be out of ink, but I made it write anyway (I'd be damned if I was going to' let another opportunity like this pass me by! I thought!). Friday night came and as usual, I had to do some checking last minute on my computer at work and sure enough, I would have to make it to my father's house immediately after work at 11:00pm to make the 12:00am-midnight phone call to Australia, where it would be around 11:00am their time

I had told her about my interview and how big it was and how important it was to me and she agreed to be ready and that we'd leave at exactly 11:00pm in order for me to make my scheduled interview time of 12:00am-Midnight. I drove home and dropped a friend off and then tore off out of the driveway for Lambertville and my Dad's house and my impending interview with Kostya Tsyzu.

I chose my dad's mainly because my Dad is who got me into boxing in the first place and anytime that I can get him to speak with any of the boxers he liked; I did so...this was one of those times. I set up my tape recorder and after much fusing and fighting to get the machine to work and record the conversation (and even more frustration getting the right phone numbers! Arggh!) we were both ready! The phone rang at exactly midnight and after letting my Dad speak directly to Kostya (come on now, you didn't think I'd let a world champion boxer not speak to my Dad, now did you?) I began my interview, these are the results of that interview.

KOSTYA TSZYU
"THE DESTINY OF A CHAMPION!"

B.D. How's your health and family?

K.T. "Good! The children just finished school; the boys are starting school again, which is good. Because, two weeks at home is too much for us to handle."

B.D. How are you adjusting to life in Australia? I know you've been there awhile.

K.T. "This is my country right now, were not thinking of moving back. I mean, Russia's always going to be my country, my homeland…But this is home right now for me."

B.D. What are you currently doing with your time?

K.T. "I've been doing lots of promotions right now, where I can spend time with my fans, doing lots of things for my sponsors and train other people now…manage other young kids and give them the right advice."

B.D. How's you injury coming along? I understand you were injured not that long ago.

K.T. "I'm very happy with the process of recovery I thought the period of inactivity would be longer for me. But, I don't like to stay sitting in a chair doing nothing…so I'm ready really. I'll start heavy exercises, in another month I'll be ready to do some heavy stuff.'

B.D. Our readers would like to know, what was it like growing up in Russia?

K.T. "It's very hard to explain if you've never been in Russia, it's probably impossible to understand. I grew up in a little town called Serov, its right in the middle of nowhere rally. It's a very little town maybe 100,000 people, very industrial…lots of pollution and its very boring for the young kids there and there's nothing else for them to do except sports. And that's probably one of the reasons why my Father put me in the gym. To calm down my activity…as a kid I was very active and secondly, for tying to keep me off of the streets and I think he succeeded with this."

B.D. Could you tell some stories about growing up, are there any that really stick out in your mind?

K.T. "Um, as a young kid…I think I was very calm…I mean, in the beginning I was very active, that's one of the reasons why my Father put me in the gym because I couldn't sit in one place for more than one second. But I'd never been very cheeky to those who are older, I always been very respectful and that's how I grew up with respect. With respect for my sport and that's what I teach my kids now, respect for everything, respect for those things around you."

B.D. You mean, in terms of respect for life, goals…things of that nature?

K.T. "Respect… Like, not to take life for granted."

B.D. What is the amateur program in Russia like? Many Americans are not really aware of it.

K.T. "I think at that time we had a great system…only the strongest survive…I mean, we had a big population…and to reach the level of the national team is very, very hard ad then when you reach it… and you want to stay there…it's even harder. Because when you are defending your national title everyone comes looking for you. As a junior, I was five time national champion and once I was second in my first year in '88. I was second in a tournament and I lost to a guy named Orzubek Nazarov, who would go on to become lightweight champion as a professional. But we still could qualify for the Olympics that season and I was in a better position... I beat nearly everybody and Nazarov had injured himself just prior to the Olympics. It put me in the number one spot which we were very proud of, which put me on an Olympic team and I was very young, only 18 and gave me a great experience and then from 1989 to '91 I really dominated my division and every year it became easier and easier for me. In '91 before the '92 Olympics I decided turn pro because I had reached the top of the amateur sport. You know, when you reach the top you usually go down and I didn't want to do that, I wanted to improve my career so '92 is a turning point where I turned to the professional ranks. It was then that I moved to Australia to fight as a professional."

B.D. Now, when you fought Nazarov in the amateur's how did that fight come off?

K.T. "We fought twice...The first time, I lost a close decision in '88 furing the final and then in '89 during the next final...I beat him...I stopped him in his hometown...and was for him...it was big shock... he was very much the favorite. I think, he was four-time national champion, very mature and he though he was gonna win. But at that time, I was in the greatest condition for the national title and in that same tournament, I fought Artur Grigorian...who would go on to become the WBO champion and recently lost to Frietas. That tournament was very good from me...as I said; three of the five guys couldn't go the distance with me."

B.D. What do you feel are the differences between the way they trained you in Russia and in an American or International style?

K.T. "The main difference being that we used to spend around 250days in the training camps away from the city, our friends and family... we only focused on one thing to do. We had loots of international competition, constantly practicing and we had lots of coaches looking after us, lots of physicians, we had a big team of scientists working for us. We had big advantages against other countries and we were paid like professionals, like sports instructors, we had great support from the government that's why we were paid like professionals, like sports instructors, we had great support from the government that's why we were very strong."

B.D. Speaking of strength, when did you first notice your incredible punching power? Was it evident from the beginning or did it just kind of happen?

K.T. "You know, I never really thought that I had huge power… Even in the beginning of my career as a kid, majority of my fights came by TKO and not really KO, because usually I was very accurate with my punching. Because I was so accurate with my punching that the referee had no choice but to stop the fights. I do remember from my first knockout, where I really knocked someone out, I knocked the bloke out, I was weighing 40 kilograms at the time and it was very scary. When someone the same size as you is falling and they can't get up. It was shock for me…but then, it became normal really"

B.D. Did you have any street fights as a kid?

K.T. "Not many, and I've usually been strong enough mentally to avoid any situations like this, some people are fighting to prove something and I never really need to prove to anybody how strong I am and ambitious. I never really was a street kid or violent, and I've always been against violence. I prefer to talk the talk and not have to do any actions. Because you really need to be professional and there's a very big chance you can damage your hands in a street fight. If you damage your hands before competition where you need to be 100 percent and you can't because you're injured by a stupid way. I'm sure many athletes regret things after a street fight.

B.D. Now, did you serve in the Russian army at all?

K.T. "Ah, yes, the Russian army has compulsory thing s where at 17, even athletes, as a system, we have to go through this and that's what we did. But for me, it was part of training camp, really. I spent a few days in there in the beginning and then it was on to the national training camps. I was very glad and two years as far as I was supposed to go and I was in there I think, 30 days…which is not bad."

B.D. No not bad at all. What did you do for fun there?

K.T. "As I said, nothing really…it wasn't very happy for me there's nothing really to do there, it was mostly training camp."

B.D. Could you tell your American fans about your Destiny DVD documenting your career and I also understand that you run your own web site www.kostyatszyu.com?Could you tell us a little bit about that as well?

K.T. "We had done this Destiny DVD prior to my unification bout, what we call "Destiny" where I won my three world titles in a tow against Diobletos Hurtado for the vacant title and then against Sharmba Mitchell where I unified the WBA and WBC titles and then Number 3 is against Zab Judah, the unification bout where I made history by being the first guy to unify the super lightweight title in more than 30 years. And it's not just the three fights themselves it's also commentary with myself, Johnny Lewis and Paul Upham. What happens behind the scenes, behind every fight. We talk about the circumstances, the pressures, from opponents, managers, the promoters…and we really talk about the historical significance of these fights. These are the really interesting things because, your usually watching the fight and you're not aware of what went on before, during, and after the fight. And that's the beauty of this DVD you can actually hear and see my commentary and thoughts on these fights and what went through my mind before, during, and after each of these historical fights."

B.D. Now, in reference to the "Destiny" DVD, did you ever feel that you were "special" or "chosen" by God to fulfill a certain destiny? Is that something that you think sometimes?

K.T. "I do think this sometimes… But sometimes I question and ignore this feeling and try and tell myself 'come on you're just normal…like everybody else.' But sometimes I see the eyes of the people around me and I do think that yeah I can't be really normal…and I'm probably not normal. And there's something moving within my life that's not normal… That's beyond normality. I believe, that I need to recognize this to myself without believing it."

B.D. And just try and keep yourself in check?

K.T. "Yes… But, what I want other people to notice is that I don't want to change and I don't think that I have changed toward other people throughout my years. I have friends that I met when I first came to Australia and I have friends from many years ago in Russia who are still friends with me now."

B.D. Now, I understand that you have special ways of training using things 'kettle balls' and 'Chinese hand balls,' can you tell our readers a little bit about them both?

K.T. "Russian kettle balls, is a special, unique, exercise coming from Russia, used by generations of Russian people. I mean I still want to find out what the record is for carrying…actually you can use these for leaping and juggling like they do in the Russian circus. You can see some o them using the Russian kettle balls, they're really great attractions. They look simple, but when you lift tem you say oh' Jesus they're heavy! They give you great stamina for your whole body and when you start exercising with them you realize in a short time that you've become so strong!"

B.D. Now the Chinese hand balls, are they something that you use to increase your punching power?

K.T. "It's not really punching power…it's not just Chinese hand balls, it's also a combination of herbs and Bo Bering's way of hitting with the internal power in your hands. I mean, I hit hard now…I've always hit hard and now I'm hitting harder than ever. It's a normal problem for boxers to damage the hands and in the beginning of my professional career my hands were always bruised, not broken but always badly bruised. Since I started using this exercise program for the last seven years I've never have a problem with my hands. That's the beauty of this exercise program I can smash the walls without feeling anything or breaking anything in my hands. For the new generation of boxers it's just unbelievable…this exercise program and we try to put this out now for the public to use. With me hitting hard and using this stuff and you don't damage yourself it's just amazing."

B.D. And you can buy these through your web site?

K.T. "I think you will be able to buy these through my web site very shortly, working on a bottle right now so it looks great and is sellable. And it works and I know it works, it needs not to just work it needs to look good as well."

B.D Now what he been doing for conditioning? As far as running and stuff?

K.T. "I've just been training every day, I've been off from the fight more than a year, but I can say I've been in the gym nearly every day. I've been done one training session every day all my life, all the time even when I'm in a resting session. And on just keeping myself strong physically and mentally because when you start preparing for any fight, you know you have this great foundation behind you."

B.D. Now, how many miles to think you run in a day?

K.T. "Right now…not a lot…I usually run about 4, 5, 6, kilometers a day. Plus weights, a little bit of back work and some light stretching."

B.D. Is there anything that you do for speed and especially for your punching power,, which you think nobody else does?

K.T. "I do some…But I think, this should stay a secret until I completely retire myself…And then I will make it available for the public to see. You don't want to give your opponents the recipe for your success."

B.D. Now, to move on to a different subject, How are things going for you financially and what's going on with the Tszyu Boxing Academy in Australia?

K.T. "Things are going good at the boxing academy, we have some good youngsters fighting her, we've only been four years in the business… starting from scratch. We got the boys themselves from scratch really, we got one boy who will qualify for the Olympic Games this year for Australia and we got a couple boys in the professional ranks. We just started developing, I don't really get to spend as much personal time with the boys, due to my schedule, but now with my injury I'll be able to spend more time now."

B.D. How are you doing financially now?

K.T. "Look…being a year and a half off from the fight business doesn't help and all my legal problems are in the past. It's just one of those things after all those many, many, years of struggling with all those court cases…it's all over now. I'm just hoping that everything goes good. Everything is going to be much easier now. Unfortunately, I made a mistake in the past. I'm thinking all is positive, everything happens for a reason in life and you become much wiser and you can give the right advice to young kids in the future who are following you and your example. Hoping that, they don't make the same mistakes that you did."

B.D. Let's talk of little bit about your fights now, tell us about some of the early fights, what was it like fighting Juan LaPorte?

K.T. "At that time…as a kid…they say 'you are going to fight Juan LaPorte, a former world champion.' I said to them 'Okay, show me the tape please.' They gave me the tape, I watched it and said 'No problem, I'll fight him.' I was very, very, confident, I thought at that time that I would fight anybody…without any preparation…and that's what I did. I really, had very great amateur background and a great deal of knowledge in the sport, I had over 270 fights as an amateur and I thought that I could fight anybody and that's what I did. With

LaPorte it wasn't really a big task, because in the first or second round I hit him to the body and from that moment on he moved backwards only and didn't really want to fight. But with a fighter like LaPorte, a former world champion, he has a lot of personal pride and with boxing you make one mistake you're gone."

B.D. What about the Larrimore fight?

K.T. "That was in the pyramid of Memphis, TN, that time again, we came to America for the first time and I didn't know who I was going to fight…they didn't give me an opponent. I didn't really know what was going on there then and as I said, I would've fought anybody then. I come to the weigh-in and I was the first time I actually saw my opponent, it was much like an amateur tournament. I just destroyed him completely, from the first minute of the fight it was one punch after another and I knocked him out in the second round I think."

B.D. Tell us about the Bramble fight?

K.T. "Against Livingston Bramble it was a great experience, a very tough guy, who was still active as a fighter and he came to really win. He thought that I was just a kid…which I was. He talked, great boxer for the promoter, he was very sellable., he talks a lot and he's selling the tickets and that's what we needed. Again, in the first or second round I hit him to the body and from what he said that he didn't want to fight me again. Like I said he's very dangerous, he threw a lot of hard punches, but it was all one way from the beginning. Even though I couldn't stop him, my hands were very bruised because he's so tough. But it was a great experience to fight a 10 round fight against great opposition."

B.D. Now, how about Hector Lopez, tell me about that fight?

K.T. "That fight was a big lesson for me, it taught me a great big lesson…didn't fight until you're prepared. I was not prepared for that fight at all…I had about 20 or 30 rounds of sparring total, I did not run because I had an injured leg and I thought the fight goes 5 or

10 rounds who cares? I had a lot of problems before that fight and I went into that fight without any preparation and the first three rounds were easy. It was easy, and I was doing everything that I knew I was supposed to do and from round 3 on I went back to my corner and I said to my trainer 'I'm tired.' I t was round three and I was already tired. Rounds 4, 5, 6 and 7 were very close rounds----out of these four rounds I lost probably three. After the seventh round I think I said to myself 'you can either give up or keep going.' And I pushed myself probably more than I could have or should have and in rounds 8, 9 and 10 I really push myself, I was very dominating. But it taught me an important lesson and it showed me what professional boxing is all about. My hands were bruised, all my body was sore, I was sick for a couple of days and I had to make a promise to myself, 'never to do this again' and 'I don't ever want to feel this way again.' And from that fight I became a professional athlete."

B.D. What about Angel Hernandez, in that fight what happened?

K.T. "It was a good fight, against a guy that fought Chavez and was stopped in …I think the sixth round for no reason really, and was great opposition for me. I knocked him down in the first round badly and he fought very well for another seven rounds and in the seventh round, I cut him with the right hand. I think and the fight was stopped because of this."

B.D. We're going to' move forward a little bit to the Phillips fight, I think that you relied more on your power and did less boxing as a result?

K.T. "Without making any excuses for myself, It wasn't me it wasn't me there…It was like a different person in there that night. I mean anybody that was watching that fight would look and say 'well, that's not Kostya Tszyu.' Again, to try and look back and find the reasons and I'd make no excuse but I made the wrong preparation at that particular time I had a lot of distractions outside the ring…court cases and other big problems…I wasn't really concentrating on the fight…I was thinking about different matters. I also started using a new diet for that particular fight for the first time I started using amino acids… without really knowing why I'm doing this and it didn't help me and I was fatigued throughout the fight. It was also the first time I was ever hit and hurt, usually when I get hit hard…it's not hurting…because I've learned to block my pain and at that particular time I could not physically control myself and had pain during this fight. I always say thank you to Vince because I learned so much in the fight and from that fight forward I became who I'm supposed to be…from that day forward I became more of a professional boxer and a professional athlete."

B.D. What about the next Sharmba Mitchell fight…will that ever come off?

K.T. "I think so…I think still everything is going well, I haven't seen the papers yet that the promoter's signed with Sharmba…so I can't really comment much more on this. I haven't signed anything myself, but I know I'm prepared to fight Sharmba Mitchell. The IBF gave me an exception to fight until November…so come November…I'll be ready. We already spoke with Showtime I think, they have me for the first week of November and I'll be ready for this particular date and I will prepare and I will be better than ever."

B.D. What about a fight with Arturo Gatti or Ricky Hatton?

K.T. "Well, look…I'd always wanted to fight Arturo Gatti and many times we thought this was going to happen but you know the problem when HBO and Showtime try to deal with each other when one fighter fights for one and the other fighter fights for the other. If nobody can come to any conclusions then we won't fight…it's as simple as that. I mean, I would love to move up in weight and fight Spinks if they can put it together."

B.D. You beat former welterweight champion Vernon Forrest in the amateurs I believe?

K.T. "Yes. It was in finals of the world amateur championships."

B.D. What about Ricky Hatton or Vernon Forrest?

K.T. "Vernon Forest is 154 now and the jump from 140 is too much and I think realistically and I had beaten him in the amateurs and he's fighting under HBO. Now Ricky Hatton's a different story, he's with Showtime, he's going to have a big crowd in Manchester and even the Showtime people would be happy to go there. But like I said 'why should I have to go there?' I mean, first of all, I need to see the prize, the money, and second of all, he needs to actually fight somebody and become the No. 1 contender. If I don't fight the No.1 contender, than I lose one of my titles and part of being a champion of the world. When he becomes No. 1 contender in the world…beautiful…let's move on."

B.D. What was the toughest fight of your career?

K.T. "Two of them, the Lopez and Phillips fight's both of them actually changed something in myself, changed my direction or opened my eyes to other things around me."

B.D. Who do you think hit the hardest?

K.T. "Hum… (thinking) Urkle…he was a heavy puncher, Zab had fast hands…not heavy…not heavy…very fast. I think Lopez has a very heavy hands…I have very damaging hands, they're a little different."

B.D. Who hit you the hardest?

K.T. "I don't really get hit that hard, except maybe in the Phillips fight when I got hurt in the fight and I was knocked down…It was painful."

B.D. How do you think you would have done against an Aaron Pryor? Or any other all-time greats?

K.T. "Oh! Against Aaron Pryor would be a very interesting fight because he threw so many wild crazy punches at you. It's so hard for me to judge myself against other great champions like Aaron Pryor. I mean, watching him as a kid and just admiring his ability to do something so unbelievable, I don't really want to comment on this myself. It's not really me to say this."

B.D. Did you have any heroes growing up in boxing? Any great fights that you like?

K.T. "I grew up in a country you really didn't have a lot of opportunities to see many great fights, but I was always a big fan of Leonard's... his great fights with Duran, Hearns and Hagler...all these fights were really great and also the great Muhammad Ali. They only showed us the fights of the guys who are very, very, popular when we were on the national team."

B.D. What about a second fight with Phillips to cap off your career?

K.T. "I don't really see it as something to prove some people may think of it in terms of revenge that I got beyond that loss and went on to became undisputed champion of the world. That was my revenge to me not to anyone else and I always say thank you to Vince for all I learned in that fight. Vince's now 42 or 43 he's lost how many fights now? How many times has he used drugs and then disqualified? The k-1? I just don't see this fight happening."

B.D. Who do you think is the greatest fighter you ever saw?

K.T. "When I look in the past, some of the boxers that I like...everyone talks about Ray Robinson and some of the things that you see him doing is beyond understanding. Some things he did in the past are unbelievable and made him such a unique person and of course Muhammad Ali the way he did things, the way he punch, the way he conduct himself...he was unique. In the modern era Roy Jones is a great, great, athlete and a great ambassador as well. As a role model for the sport, I think Oscar is a great ambassador with what he did, he is really great for the sport."

B.D. Would there ever be a match-up between you and Oscar De La Hoya? It was always such a big super fight?

K.T. "Before the lose to Vince Phillips there was the opportunity and possibility that we were going to fight. But now that Oscar weighs about 160 pound, I can't see this fight happening. Because, probably after his next fight, Oscar will probably retire, because he's already made history, in the way that nobody else will ever do it again."

B.D. So have you Kostya, you both have done it.

K.T. "Unfortunately…I have not been active in my last three years here because of injuries and one of the reasons that I have not retired is because I want to prove that not this injury or anything else son stop me and to finish my destiny."

B.D. What's in the future for Kostya Tszyu? What do you see yourself doing?

K.T. "I will probably follow in Oscar's footsteps and create a promotional company to look after some Australian boys and some Russian boys in the Soviet Union's republics. Because I have great connection up there and who knows? I'm going to Russia next week in Moscow, to launch my new sports drink, the Tszyu Drink. That is made in Russia from the berries in the place where I grew up eating these same berries in Serov Russia. It can be good business for me in the future and I'm sure you will see the Tsyzu drink in America as well.

K.T. "We fought in the same competition in 1990 at the Goodwill Games, I won the Goodwill Games when I beat Terrance Millet in the semifinal, Mosley fought in the lightweight division and he fought one weight smaller than me, so we never met.

"The first time that Oscar ever fought in big time international fight was in Seattle, Washington, when he won the Goodwill Games in his weight class and we have been friends for a very long time."

B.D. Did you and Oscar ever spar together as amateurs?

K.T. "No we never sparred, but our lives have never been that different, in Russia they call me Golden Boy."

B.D. Apt description, now can you tell all you fans and all the people out there who read Boxing Digest a little bit about your "Destiny" video and how they can get in through your website?

K.T. "When you log into my website which is www.kostyatszyu.com, you got to section marked store to find the spot marked Destiny DVD and you click on it. There you will find lots of merchandise from me…books, gloves, t-shirts, lots of Tszyu merchandise. So you log into our forum and join up for free and I think it is one of the best boxing forums in the world."

B.D: Nice, Anything you want to say to your millions of fans out there who read Boxing Digest?

K.T. "I'm reading my website every single day and I'm very happy to see so many American fans out there, I haven't been in the states now for awhile. So I'm very happy when I read these great things they write and say about me and they all still remember me and they still recognize me as one of the best… it makes me very pleased. To them I say thanks and I want very much to come to the States on a promotional tour and meet my fans there and join with them."

"POST-FIGHT"

Kostya would go on to defend the championship against Sharmba Mitchell again, knocking him out even easier this time and the boxing world was stunned by Kostya's accomplishment. My interview with Kostya went to press the month before their fight and I honestly hope that, maybe it helped to build up their fight a bit. After that, another jr. welterweight, Ricky Hatton was calling out Tsyzu's name (see the very next chapter on my interview and story with Ricky Hatton!). Tsyzu defeated Mitchell, like he did so many others before him and Tszyu was left sitting on top of the world and I, thank god, had gotten my opportunity to interview him. To God, I am, forever thankful!

RICKY HATTON INTERVIEW
"PRE-FIGHT"
"THE CURRENT PRIDE OF GREAT BRITAIN!"

For those of you who don't know who Ricky Hatton is, by the time you read this, he will have had become the world champion in both the junior-welterweight division as well, as the welterweight division, within the sport of boxing. Hatton is a short undefeated, compact, left hooker, from Manchester England, with an excruciating left hook to the body, which paralyzed opponents and stopping them right in their tracks. Again, I don't feel like I can ever express enough thanks to my editor, Greg Juckett, who'd given me the contact for Ricky Hatton's manager and basically, gotten me this interview that you're currently reading. I had called Hatton's manager, through Sky Sports in England and the receptionist had gotten me through to him and he answered, with the thickest cockney English accent you ever heard! Let me give you the reader a quick re-cap of what our five-minute conversation sounded like, I said nothing and I heard even less of what he said, except for what sounded like, "right en, I'll ave Ricky ready on, bout' four-thirty, ensday, okay?" To which I said, Okay...I'll be ready!" This, I then took to mean "he'll have Ricky ready about four-thirty on Wednesday, okay????" Now, the only problem was to call at four thirty, I'm at my apartment and Wednesday roles around and I get ready to call Ricky Hatton's house, the phone rings halfway across the Atlantic and I get...Ricky's dad...with an even thicker cockney accent than Ricky's manager had! I spoke with the elder, Mr. Hatton, for about fifteen minutes before I got out of him that, "Ricky, was at the gym sparring and he wouldn't be back until late. Oh' and by the way, the interview was set for Thursday, not Wednesday as I had previously thought." Oh' well, I figured, at least I know enough now from my previous interview with Kostya Tsyzu's people, to know to call people from across the ocean in their actual time zones! So, Thursday roles around and I finally get a hold of young, Mr. Ricky Hatton. It was a great interview for me, with a fighter who I thought would *at least,* go on to become a great, all-action fighter, if not a champion. At the time that this interview was done, Ricky was the mandatory challenger for both the IBF junior-welterweight belt held by Kostya Tsyzu and the WBO junior-welterweight belt, held by Miguel Cotto and after my last interview with Tsyzu, it was announced that Tsyzu would indeed, defend his IBF welterweight belt against Ricky Hatton on June, 5th 2005. So, it was a safe bet that this fight would at least come off and be made and interviewing Ricky (who's an all-action fighter) was what the public wanted to read about and that's what I really expected. What I didn't expect, was the absolute certainty that Ricky spoke with about actually defeating Tsyzu, never before, had I spoken with a fighter who was set for an upcoming fight that spoke with as much certainty about defeating his opponent (most of which I couldn't write or print, just in case he lost) as Ricky Hatton did about defeating Kostya Tsyzu. It wasn't so much what Hatton said *about Tsyzu,* it was *the way he said it.* During the course of our interview, he would often speak about, "After defeating Tsyzu for the title…or …after I win the belt' I'll probably, just…" without a hint of brashness like Ali or the straight up cockiness like Pernell Whitaker did, no, Ricky spoke about defeating Tsyzu for the title, with such absolute belief and sincerity in this event, in such a way, that I actually began to believe, that he had already won and defeated Tsyzu myself! I now believe, that at the time of this interview, Ricky Hatton had the idea, dream and image of the defeat of Kostya Tsyzu by himself, Ricky Hatton, so firmly entrenched in his visual mind, that going to the fight, was nothing more than an afterthought for him. I came away awestruck by his conviction and complete determination in himself and after I put the phone down after the interview with Ricky Hatton, I could only come away, proud and inspired.

THE HIT MAN'S GUNNING FOR KOSTYA TSZYU!

by
Richard Scurti

BD: Ricky, How are things going right now?

RH: Things are going great right now, I'm the #1 mandatory contender for Miguel Cotto's belt and I'm the mandatory for Kostya Tsyzu's IBF belt, as well. So things are looking good and I'm doing really well. Hopefully, I'll be set to face Kostya Tsyzu June 5th and I can look forward to all those years of hard work paying off and I'll get my shot at Kostya Tszyu and I can prove once again that I'm the number-one best fighter in the division. I just had my last fight around Christmas time and I look to forward to my upcoming fight with Kostya Tsyzu.

BD: Ricky, A lot of our American readers don't know a lot about you; can you tell us how you got started in boxing?

RH: I did kickboxing when I was about eight years old and I was very short and stocky and I wasn't very talented with my feet; but I was with my fists. So, I went to a local boxing club at eleven years old and no one else ever dreamed to get this far with boxing. My father and me were both more into football or rugby as you call it than boxing and he used to play for the Manchester City football team; American fans are probably more familiar with the Manchester United football team that are featured in the movie "Euro Trip". But, that's what I really wanted to do was to play football rather than boxing and follow in my father's footsteps.

BD: Yes, you actually remind me of a former jr. welterweight contender a bit in Dave "Boy", Green, do you remember him?

RH: Yes, actually, I speak with Dave every now and again and he was one of my favorite fighters growing up. I spoke to Dave not that long ago and he always calls to wish me good luck and such; he was such a brave man, a very good fighter.

BD: Great, now out of everybody out there what would be your "hit list", as least as far as possible opponents go?

RH: Well' as I said before, I'd really like to fight Kostya Tsyzu first, because Tsyzu is considered the best in the division now with that second very convincing win over Sharmba Mitchell. I'm his number one contender and now that the fight has been set for over here in the U.K. I really want to prove that I'm the very best in the division.

BD: What about Gatti? Would you ever consider taking a fight with Arturo Gatti if that fight could be made regardless after you fight Kostya Tsyzu?

RH: Definitely! Me and Gatti would also be one hell of a fight, with two great warriors in there in the ring, with no bullshit in the ring; it would be a real barnstormer of a fight. I would definitely love to fight him as well, I feel I can beat him and a win like that over Arturo Gatti would prove that I'm the very best in the division. Of course, there's also Miguel Cotto who I'm also the mandatory for his WBO belt, a fighter who is on the tips of everybody's lips at the moment, I'd like to get my shot at fighting Miguel Cotto after fighting Kostya Tsyzu. You have Floyd Mayweather in there as well, who I'd also like to fight; just a lot of fantastic matches out there for me, in the junior-welterweight division at this time.

BD: Now, on a different note, you come out to a rather peculiar theme song, "Blue Moon" where and how did that come about for your ring entrance?

RH: There's a very small group here in Manchester called Supra not very well known and they sing that song, "Blue Moon" as the theme of Manchester City Football team and with me grand dad played for

Britain's main sport, too. I thought I'd come to the ring with their shirt on and the song playing. They're the most beloved City soccer team and I'd like to make them just as famous for coming out to play on the field, as I get for fighting in the boxing ring; so that's where that song comes from really.

BD: You have your own website www.rickyhitmanhatton.com I believe, can you tell your American fans a little bit about it? Also, how they can get in contact with you?

RH: Yeah, as you stated, I've got me own website www.rickyhitmanhatton.com like a lot of fighters these days and you can get the latest info on me and Manchester City. It's all very, very, big business now and I'm just glad to really let people know about it and how they can contact me.

BD: Ricky, how do you really see yourself in the future? What're your future plans?

RH: I would just like to get my shot at Kostya Tszyu, I've had thirty-eight fights all wins and I'm only twenty-six years old, I'm not even at my peak yet and I really feel and would also like all my fans to know that, the best is yet to come.

BD: What's been your toughest fights so far?

RH: Probably either the Ben Tackie or Vince Phillips fights, they were both strong and stayed very dangerous throughout the whole fight really.

BD: Would you ever consider moving up to welterweight?

RH: No, not at the moment I'm kind of a big junior-welterweight and I don't foresee it happening now, there's too much fighting in this division.

BD: What have you been doing as far as working out?

RH: Well, you look at the longevity of fighters like Bernard Hopkins and Oscar De La Hoya and they both have conditioners and nutritionists and the like so I decided to do the same. Where I do more roadwork and training and just watch my food intake and what not.

BD: Who hit you the hardest?

RH: Both Ben Tackie or Vince Phillips, I made Tackie miss a lot and he didn't catch me right, but I could feel that he was very strong even as the fight wore on. Vince Phillips is also a very strong puncher, during the fight he was crafty and he did hit me with a right uppercut in round four and I definitely felt that so, he *can* hit. But, I have much confidence with my chin, you can't really expect to fight and think that you can be hurt but I've never felt very out on my feet at all.

BD: Who would you say you hit the hardest thus far? Any other tough fights?

RH: There was a kid in Detroit, a top ten fighter named Gilbert Quiros who I boxed in Detroit and knocked out in the second round, but he was very dangerous, very explosive puncher and he fell like a tree that was chopped down really. Ambioris Figuero, I knocked him out in four rounds and I never hit someone so hard in my life really, it was one of my better knockouts really.

BD: Being from Britain, who were some of your favorite British fighters and where do you see yourself in their standing as of right now?

RH: well you have Nigel Benn possibly one of the best most exciting fighters to ever come out of Britain, Naseem Hamed, also very exciting and did a lot to popularize the sport here and I would like to be one of them as well, win one of the titles from Kostya Tsyzu and defend my title against the very best in the world.

BD: What about Lennox Lewis?

RH: Without a doubt, you can't think of great fighters and not think of Lennox, he's one of the best really; he belongs up there with the great ones. I always enjoyed the all-time greats, some of my favorite fighters are Roberto Duran, Dave Green, Sugar Ray Leonard, Chavez, and I would like for my fight with Kostya Tsyzu to define my greatness and put me up there with the great ones.

BD: Great, any final words to your millions of global fans, who read Boxing Digest?

RH: Absolutely, I got a fantastic fan base here in England particularly Manchester and I know all of Manchester and the whole country will be rooting for me when I beat Kostya Tsyzu for the title on June 5th and I would like to be as popular in the United States as I am here. With me beating Tsyzu, I hope my American fan base will grow and support me and I know they'll enjoy watching me. I may have a small following in the U.S. but American fans will see after the Tsyzu fight, that my fights carry a lot of great value for your money and after Kostya Tsyzu and if this fight can be made, look forward to me fighting Arturo Gatti next! I just want to thank everyone; my mum and dad, my trainer, my promoter, Frank Warren, and everybody that helped to get me, where I am today, I won't let you down and come June 5th you won't be disappointed!"

POST-FIGHT:

Like I said, in retrospect, I had never come across a fighter who was that sure of himself. He spoke of beating Tszyu like it was bound to happen, *like it was destined to happen.* Remember, we're talking about a great world champion, who had held his crown for almost seven years defeating and knocking out the very best fighters, that America and the world could muster…Ricky spoke of his defeating Tszyu like it was something, which would happen, in due course. Ricky Hatton would go on to defeat the great, Kostya Tsyzu by tko in the 11th round, on June 5th 2005 and as Ricky predicted, *"Tsyzu was never really in the fight."* After that historic win, he would surprise me and the rest of the world, by going up in weight to welterweight and lifting the welterweight title from Luis Callazzo in twelve hard-fought rounds (a fight more than a few observers thought he barely won, if at all). In doing so, Ricky Hatton has done his life's part by becoming a two-time, two division world boxing champion and in the process, has already made himself into the boxing legend that he'd predicted to me back in 2005. As of this moment, Ricky is set to fight the new, world welterweight kingpin, Floyd Mayweather and whether he wins or loses, Ricky Hatton has already done, what so many other boxers only dream of doing, becoming a world champion and ultimately, a boxing legend."

BERNARD HOPKINS INTERVIEW PRE-FIGHT:

In October 2004, I was lucky enough to go with my editor, Greg Juckett and some friends, down to the WBO and IBO conference' in Miami, Florida. At that time, Bernard Hopkins was the undisputed middleweight champion of the world (he was the only man who had just knocked out both Felix Trinidad and Oscar De La Hoya all during eighteen title defenses, an all-time middleweight record and he'd be less than three years away from winning the world light-heavyweight title in addition to the middleweight title) and nobody had interviewed him in quite awhile. At that time, the boxing world was hearing whispers of Oscar De La Hoya signing Bernard Hopkins to become a partner in his new promotional company, Golden Boy Productions. It was being whispered that that particular announcement would be made sometime in November. I wasn't entirely sure myself...however, Bernard was already considered an all time great boxer and I figured that a really great interview with Bernard Hopkins, could potentially put me in line to interview Oscar De La Hoya himself...if...he were to sign Bernard as his new "partner" as was currently being rumored. I had the distinct pleasure to interview Bernard Hopkins after his knockout defense of Oscar De La Hoya...these are my results.

BERNARD HOPKINS: THE UNDISPUTED BEST!

By
Richard Scurti

BD: Bernard how'd you get started in boxing?
BH: I grew up in Philly watching a lot of local heroes like Bennie Briscoe fight, I was very impressed with him as a fighter and as a man... he was a real technician. When you're growing up with all the brothers in my family and you have to fight to get your meals before they do, then you learn how to fight!

BD: Where do you see yourself as an all-time great middleweight champion?
BH: There was three middleweight legends, Ray Robinson, Carlos Monzon, and Marvin Hagler, I would just like to be considered as also one of the great middleweight champions of all time, it doesn't really matter to me as to where I am on that list... as long as I'm considered.

BD: How do you feel about breaking Carlos Monzon's record?
BH: Monzon was a real man and a great champion, I spent ten years of my life trying to tie and then break that record and he was an excellent fighter, a tall, technician with a strong right hand and there was no running from him.

BD: What was your toughest fight?
BH: Two of them for two very different reasons; Roy Jones and Sergundo Mercado. They were both tough, because with Roy I felt I had the edge in the fight and I spent a lot of time after that thinking about what I would do right if we were to fight again, I felt that I won that fight and that he slipped away. Sergundo Mercado was just a tough, strong brawling fighter, he really pushed me to my limits but, he pushed everybody then.

BD: Would you still like to fight Roy Jones again?
BH: No' cause I don't think that the public really cares if Roy Jones fights again, he's been knocked out twice now and he really fell under the radar with that. No, I really don't care if we fight and it's not really a big money fight for me anymore... but I would like to fight the guy who knocked him out! I'll fight Glencoffe Johnson because now that I'm thinking like a promoter, I already beat Johnson knocking him out before so, let's do it again!

BD: What's in the future for you right now?
BH: To get my twenty defenses of the middleweight title and retire when I'm forty, I had promised my mother that I would retire before I turned forty and that age just feels right to me and I want to keep my promise to her. Maybe fight the winner of the Johnson/Tarver fight, but I definitely want to notch my twenty defenses first.

BD: Would you fight Felix Trinidad again?
BH: Yeah, I'll fight Trinidad again, I'll definitely take that fight, Trinidad fights an easy one-dimensional style. But he's also a great fighter, so I give him a lot of respect, he's recently shown the ability to fight backing up and he moved more in his fight with Mayorga. All while still trying to land that left hook and he's got a good right hand now, but in my heart I believe.... He can't beat me. Felix wants to fight me to redeem him self.

BD: D you think the shot you hit Oscar with was your best shot?
BH: I hurt a lot of guys with body shots in the gym and wear them down and that's my basic style. It takes a lot out of a man and I'm the type of person who would like to celebrate things later on in life, not now. So I try to take them apart piece by piece but, I know what it's like to have the wind knocked out of you and you just feel like you can't move. That fight...I'm basically bigger and stronger so it was amazing enough for him to get up the way that he did... but it would have got worse for him if he had gone on.

Richard Scurti

I had no sign of tiredness and I was getting stronger as the fight progressed and I knew I was losing so I applied the pressure and the rest now is just business.

BD: Who hit you the hardest?
BH: Antwun Echols, definitely very heavy-handed, he hits very hard.

BD: What's in the future for Bernard Hopkins?
BH: Twenty defenses, maybe against Howard Eastman for the title and my birthday falls within that time frame ... or move up to fight Johnson or just drop a little bit of weight to fight Winky Wright... so by the this time next year I can say that it's a wrap.

BD: Great, thank you for your time Bernard.
BH: Thank you.

POST-FIGHT:

Yes, I'll be the first to admit that this wasn't exactly my longest interview, but you'll have to understand that I did approach Bernard out of the blue during the 2004 WBO conference. I walked up to him from behind and he was already being swamped by people and tapped him on the shoulder. " Mr. Hopkins" I said, "could I ask you some questions…I'd like to interview you for Boxing Digest magazine?" He looked down balefully at me and looked me up and down before nodding silently and motioning with his finger for me to follow him and we sat at his table with his friends and family…he must have seen the suit I had on…and felt sorry for me. No, but seriously, I was very happy just to get this interview and I truly thank God and Bernard Hopkins everyday, for this great opportunity. As great as it was, it would only lead to greater ones for me…the best was still, yet to come.

OSCAR DE LA HOYA INTERVIEW PRE-FIGHT:

I stated in my last interview with Bernard Hopkins, there was a serious rumor going around that Bernard Hopkins was going to sign with Oscar De La Hoya as Oscar's new promotional partner, in some manner. As it turned out, Oscar *would end up* signing Bernard almost two weeks after I had interviewed Bernard Hopkins. So...I called up my great, editor, Greg Juckett...again and I asked him for Oscar's contact. As soon as I got a hold of his publicist, I immediately told her how I had just interviewed Bernard and how I really wanted to get Oscar's thoughts on his signing Bernard as the head of his new promotional company, Golden Boy East...*and how it would be free publicity (this is a great tactic for any writer hoping to break into the business...nobody turns their ears or eyes away when they hear the word, "free"...unless of course, they have a personal axe to grind with you...then don't bother, because you're screwed, anyway)* for Oscar and his newfound company. Of course, she couldn't get me an exact time but, the other part of interviewing famous people and actually getting them is in using these exact words as much as possible... "I can do the interview at any time" and "Ill just need ten minutes of so and so's time...whenever he/she is ready or available"...you'd be surprised at how often those two phrases really will actually work for you. About three days later, I got the call that I would get exactly...five minutes...to interview him...but...it was worth it. Yes, I did ask Oscar about the promotional company, but luckily...I was also able to ask him so boxing questions too, like, "who hit him the hardest" etc...below are the results.

OSCAR DE LA HOYA: THE GOLDEN BOY SPEAKS! BY RICHARD SCURTI

BD:
Oscar, what got you started in boxing?

OSCAR:
Well, I guess it was my father really, my father and grandfather both fought amateur and professional and in the beginning I didn't really like to fight. I liked baseball, you know, other sports, but it was the lureof competition really. When I saw that you could get trophies and really make a lot of money in the sport and there was that constant need to succeed and improve that drew me to boxing. With my father, brother, and grandfather fighting before me, I guess I had no choice really. (laughs)

BD:
So you feel it was the competition that interested you?

OSCAR:
Definitely, it was the competition to become the best and fighting amateur got me ready to turn pro and gave me the desire to become the best and I carried all of that with me to this day as a promoter.

BD:
Now, can you tell me a little bit about your signing with Bernard Hopkins as the head of the newly created Golden Boy East?

OSCAR:
Yes, Bernard is my partner now as head of Golden Boy Promotions

East. We both are looking forward to putting on really great, solid shows on the east coast, as well as the west coast. Right now we have the fight cards Solo Boxeo on Telefutura and Boxeo Deoro on HBO Latino and HBO PPV events as well as Grand Olympic Auditorium, MGM Grand, there's the Battle at the Ballroom at Irvine Marriott, Irvine Calif. So we are both looking to expand rapidly to give boxing fans a good show and to give them something different.

(You can get event tickets or TV listings by going to www.goldenboypromotions.com and click on schedule.)

BD:
Let's talk a little bit about your fights now, what was your toughest fight?

OSCAR:
Ike Quartey, definitely. He was very strong, a very hard puncher, just so tough. I was fighting in my fourth weight division at the time and he hit me with a right hand in the eighth round and I was like...Oh man So it was a very hard, tough, fight.

BD:
Okay, Vargas?

OSCAR:
There was bad blood before that fight, I mean, I just didn't like the guy, I respect him as a fighter. But he talked a lot of trash before the fight and there was something about him where... I just didn't like the guy as a person. He made for a lot of bad blood and I really wanted to hurt him and make him pay for it. I just really wanted to put an end to it once and for all.

BD:
How about Chavez?

Oscar:
Chavez...you know, at the time... being a young kid he was my hero. He was heading into his 100th win and me being so young I was just twenty-four at the time and here I am fighting this hero to both me and the Mexican people. But I went in there and just did my job and you know, won big. It was a very big moment for me both on a personal and a professional level.

BD:
What about Kostya Tsyzu? Why hasn't that fight ever come off?

OSCAR:
I was set to fight Kostya before he lost to Vince Phillips and it was probably going to happen. But, I ended up going in just a different direction and I'll still be fighting at 147 pounds so there's still the chance that fight could come off and I would fight him definitely. But there's a lot of great fights out there at 147 pounds so I'll have to juggle around who my opponents might be Spinks, Trinidad, or Tszyu... it's still a great fight.

BD:
Okay, Camacho?

OSCAR:
He did a lot of talking before the fight and bad mouthed me a little bit,
so I really wanted to put a beating on this guy. I really wanted to hurt him and prolong it, I just wanted to get in there and take him apart and I liked watching the blood flow. He talked so much before the fight I felt I needed to teach him a lesson and just give him a very long beating.

BD:
All right, How about Paez?

OSCAR:
With Paez I just hit him right on the button, I mean, it was just a real good shot right on the jaw and he really walked into it. As soon as I hit him...I knew it was over and he was a very good fighter.

BD:
Who would you say hit the hardest?

OSCAR:
Quartey! He throws some very hard shots and every time one of them landed it was like I was hit with a brick, the guy really threw some hard punches that felt like I was being hit with bricks. And very early in my career, I fought a guy named Mike Grable in Rochester, NY and he hit me very hard on the nose, like a sledgehammer. I put him down twice and I was very glad when it finally ended when it did.

BD:
Would you ever fight Mosley a third time?

OSCAR:
I don't think so. I mean, me and Shane are both very good friends and he's a very good guy and I just think...he's got my number. I mean, styles make fights and he's got a style that you know... nine times out of ten... his is going to beat mine. Not necessarily that he's a better fighter... but I... I...I just kind of feel that he has my number. So no, I really don't see a third fight ever coming off.

BD:
What's in the future for Oscar De La Hoya and Golden Boy Promotions?

OSCAR:
We'll still be promoting our fights the Solo Boxeo on Telefutura and Boxeo Deoro on HBO Latino along with HBO PPV. Local shows at places like Grand Olympic Auditorium, MGM Grand, there's the Battle at the Ballroom at Irvine Marriott, Irvine Calif. We'll just keep

expanding into other places and other areas really. I'm still officially active as a fighter and as of this moment I've decided to continue fighting at 147 pounds and I'll just decide on who I want to fight next.

BD:
Great, thank you for your time Oscar.

OSCAR:
Thank you, I appreciate your time and I love talking to my boxing fans.

POST-FIGHT:

As I've said before, this interview was kind of anticlimactic for me, mainly because of the short amount of time it took to actually do the interview but, it was still an accomplishment for me, nonetheless. Oscar, much like Kostya Tszyu, was another big time hero of mine growing up in the mid-1990's and much like Kostya Tszyu, I also wanted to fight with Oscar, too (but, like my dream match-up with Tszyu, Oscar would have also probably knocked my head clean off…I'd have been too brave and fought face first against him) and even though my actual boxing career never took off…it was almost exactly ten years to the day when I would meet and beat Oscar De La Hoya finally in a bout of verbal and written jousts, during the course of our interview. I always like to think that I knew that I'd face off against these guys, just not within a boxing ring. This is one of those interviews that I am immensely proud of accomplishing and I thank God for it, everyday.

CHRISTY MARTIN INTERVIEW PRE-FIGHT:

Around the summer of 2004, I was lucky enough to go with my Dad (who had gotten me into boxing in the first place) to the Boxing Hall of Fame again in Canostota, New York. During the course of the parade, I was fortunate enough to meet with a young girl who had come up to the Hall with a guy from Vibe magazine. I was intrigued and offered to meet him and I was introduced to long running underground rap sensation, R.A. "The Rugged Man". It is because of him that these next couple of interviews, were even done and I wish to thank him for all of his help and I am eternally grateful for his help. I had seen Christy Martin, who in 1996 fought on the under card of Tyson/Bruno-II and people went wild for her and women's boxing forever afterwards. It was R.A. who had got me Christy's contact and it was because of him, that this following interview was done.

CHRISTY MARTIN
"THE COAL MINER'S DAUGHTER"

BOXING DIGEST INTERVIEWS: "CHRISTY MARTIN!"

ByRichard Scurti

For many years, the sport of Women's boxing had languished without an immediate female star to propel the sport into the public limelight. That all changed when on March 16th 1996, on the Mike Tyson/Frank Bruno-II under card that two women fought a bloody, hard fought battle in the same ring, which would put the men fighting on the card there that night to shame. A young girl named Christy Martin staged a six round brawl with Deirdre Gogarty and through a very tough fight and a very, bloody nose, Christy Martin would take a unanimous decision, in the process of winning America's hearts that night in 1996. From that fight on, Christy Martin would go on to become the Mary Lou Retton of Women's Boxing (even appearing on the cover of Sports Illustrated), while also helping to push the sport of women's boxing out into the mainstream. She became the face to consider whenever the subject of Women's Boxing would come up and is without a doubt possibly the most famous female boxer in the world today. Boxing Digest was recently granted an interview with Christy before her workout session and this is what she had to tell us.

BD: How are things going?

CM: Things are going good, you know, I'm on my way to the gym, I know I have to get back in there, I goofed around a little bit. But I'm starting to work out again and just looking forward to getting back in the gym again.

BD: So, are you still active then…you're not retiring or anything?

CM: No…no, I'm not retired…I don't know where that rumor got started from but, I'm here to tell you first that, I always said that, even before the Laila Ali fight that win, lose, or draw I was going to' continue fighting and I'm actually hoping to get another shot at Laila Ali. I feel that I can do much better than I did the first time around with Laila and I want people to know that, I always come to fight.

BD: With that in mind, what will you be doing now?CM: Well, we just had hurricane Charley sweep through here in West Virginia and knocked out a lot of power here. We just got done buying my grandmother's house and just getting back into shape takes time, running up here in the mountains again, is a whole lot different than running on the flat, gravel in Florida. (laughs)

BD: How did you get the nickname "The Coal Miner's Daughter"?

CM: Um…when I was first starting out, my husband Jim and Jimmy Lennon jr. were trying to come up with an idea to kind of give me a little bit of pizzazz and my dad and brother both worked in the coal mines and so did my grandfather and the name really just kind of… stuck. Lorreta Lynn the original, "Coal Miner's Daughter" actually called me on the phone before the Laila Ali fight to wish me luck and that was just so cool, because I am such a big fan of hers. Like I always say, that bloody nose that I got in the Gogarty fight was the most promotional bloody nose in the history of sports. (laughs)

BD: Now, aside from training, could you tell our readers what you do in your spare time?

CM: Well, like I said…I do like to stay in shape, maybe have a few tune-up fights before fighting Laila Ali again. I feel that I can beat her and I just got caught cold in that first round and wasn't able to recover fully by the fourth round and really just took my husband's advice to stay down. I knew that I wasn't going to' recover from the straight right hand that she caught me with in the first round and I remember thinking that's better to not go on and just you know…fight her again some other time. Me and my husband Jim, are also training a few fighters as well; such as, Roland Bryant 10-0 8-ko's, and Backlin Medrano who are both very good prospects themselves. I tell Jim that I want to have kids and that's something that we'd like to work on in the future and we both know…you have to deal with my biological clock running against my professional career clock too. We would like to raise my pro record up to fifty wins before I even think about retiring and after that kind of sit down and start a family.

BD: What about a match-up with arch rival Lucia Riker?

CM: Definitely! I definitely would like to fight her! We actually sat down with Lucia's promotion team for three hours before the Klitchko/Brewster fight and when I told them that I want the fight, they just stopped and we never heard from them again…it never even got to the money point.

BD: So, you guys never even got to discuss the money angle for the fight?

CM: No…like I said, it never even got to the money point and it's almost like Lucia just wanted to mess with me and see if I would jump so she could say that I backed down from it and that's not the case at all! Don King had all but signed the two of us to fight and she didn't on her end and what's more is, the public doesn't even know her! She hasn't even been that active as of late and that's her own fault.

BD: What about a second fight with Mia St. John?

CM: I would like to fight her again, if a promoter came to me right now and offered me that fight with Mia St. John, I would take it. I kind of goofed off a little bit before that last fight and didn't really train as well as I should have maybe. I actually should have done much better than I did against her and I think I probably should have knocked her out…even though, Mia surprised me by being, so tough. (laughs)

BD: What's your take on the Perfect 10 model boxing?

CM: I actually sat down with Laila at a Perfect 10 press conference to hype our upcoming fight and most of the women there were very nice and very pretty and most really tried to fight and stuff. But, I think those kind of things mostly rely on the sex and stuff to sell the fight and not really the fighters themselves. So I don't think that kind of thing really helps us out in the professional ranks, although you never know cause…some of those women might be really good fighters who just want exposure.

BD: Where do you see the sport of women's boxing going now?

CM: Women's boxing today, it just doesn't seem to have garnered as much of the same interest that it had during the early part of my career. I think that women's boxing has really fallen from where it was and there really isn't anyone to kind of take it the next level yet and bring it out and really…generate more interest in it again.

BD: Is there anything that you want to say to your millions of fans out there, who read Boxing Digest?

CM: Just to…not judge me from the Laila Ali fight…I'm a warrior and it was very difficult for me to take that…that I stopped fighting when I did. I always come to fight and I look forward to showing boxing fans that I can do better and beat Laila Ali in the rematch. I mean, so many people come up to me and say "Christy…you should have kept going, she looked so tired and I say yeah, she was tired from pounding on top of my head. (laughs) So yeah' look forward to seeing me again and I'll be back and better than I ever was for the rematch.

POST-FIGHT:

There really isn't too much to tell after this interview, I was again, very proud of interviewing such an important boxing figure and it still seems kind of surreal to me when I see her on Conan O'Brien with my wife. The opponent that I was asking Christy about, "Lucia Riker" was the boxer turned actress, who fatally injures Hilary Swank during the end of the film, "Million Dollar Baby" and I now believe that because Riker's acting aspirations...their match-up will now...never happen. Again, I can't thank R.A. enough for giving me these next couple of contacts, please, if you're reading this...go out and buy any of R.A. "The rugged Man's" albums for me...I got to give him a direct call out..."R.A., thanks, dude".

DIEGO CORRALES INTERVIEW! PRE-FIGHT:

This interview was conducted after going to the Boxing Hall of Fame again in 2005, when I saw the most attractive, Latin woman getting hot dogs at concession stand. I felt that I'd need to introduce myself after spotting the words "Corrales Family" on her name tag and for obvious reasons...I felt the need to talk to her and as it turns out, she was Diego Corrales' wife! Diego was an all-time great fighter who was in three "fight of the year" boxing matches, during an eight-year career long run. I followed Mrs. Corrales up to the dais where Diego was signing autographs and sat down to talk with him. My first impression was that he kind of reminded me of a big kid, at 5'11 and 130-145 pounds, like a string bean of a kid, Diego didn't just smile, while he sat there signing autographs...he beamed! This was a super great interview and I am very happy to have gotten this interview and I thank God for the opportunity to meet and interview this great man and fighter. Around this time, our editor Greg Juckett had informed me that our publisher of Boxing Digest now wanted all writers to interview people using a "story format" where I was to write a either fact or opinion or two followed by the persons thoughts or opinions they said to back my story up. While, these next couple of interviews *are written* in that format and style, make no mistake...these are actually interviews with real living people and in March of 2005, written below are my results of my interview with Diego Corrales.

DIEGO CORRALES SHOOTS FOR SUPER STARDOM!

By Richard Scurti

"This is what I've been waiting for" beamed a jubilant Diego Corrales as he sat next to his beautiful wife signing autographs at this year's Boxing Hall of Fame in Canastota New York. "This is what I've worked so hard for my whole life, to be able to just be here with all these all-time greats and to sit next to some of my own heroes I had while growing up… I'm just thrilled to be here."

Indeed, Diego Corrales does have a lot to be thankful for, after being in what should be considered a definite shoe in for Fight of the Year with his tenth round TKO victory over Jose Luis Castillo, no one knows more about thrills right now, than Diego Corrales. After pulling himself up off the floor twice in the tenth round, Diego thrilled the audiences both at home and especially at ringside, when he came back from the brink of what looked like certain defeat after being floored so badly (Diego's mouthpiece actually popped out of his mouth after he had hit the floor) that it seemed he would never get back up. And yet, somehow Diego dug down deep inside and stood up to go on and land some heavy shots of his own that had Castillo drunk against the ropes. "That was the toughest fight of my career," exclaimed Corrales "I knew I'd get back up but, he was very strong and probably the hardest puncher I've faced so far."

Diego knows a lot about coming back from what looks like certain defeat, he came back from a one-sided loss to the now, three-weight division champion Floyd Mayweather jr. back in 2001 following alleged charges by his ex-wife of spousal abuse. Diego knows a lot about digging down deep within your soul for what *only you* think is there.

After all, that's what Diego must have done following the decisive loss to Mayweather when he bounced back with a series of quick confidence building wins before facing off and beating the other top two men of his division in, Acelino Freitas and Joel Cassamayor. After that came the thrilling, Castillo fight, a fight that is almost a shoe in for Fight of the Year, now you have to ask yourself… where does Diego go from here? Does he stay at lightweight and take a rematch with Castillo or does he move up to junior welterweight for a rematch with Floyd Mayweather or maybe even a potential explosive, showdown with newly crowned IBF champion Ricky Hatton?

"I'll probably be staying at lightweight" said Corrales as he signed a young kid's boxing glove from the podium at the Hall of Fame this year "Yeah' I'll fight Castillo again man' that was an excellent fight and I was proud to be in it, but the man I want to fight right now is Erik Morales, you know? If he'll move up to lightweight to fight me, I'd like to fight Morales next."

"Erik had said in couple of the newspapers that if Diego was able to beat Castillo, than *maybe* Erik would think about fighting him," explained the stunningly beautiful Mrs. Corrales as she watched her man interacting with his many fans. "Diego took a lot of offense to that comment and some other stuff that he said and now *he's the man Diego wants to fight*" said a smiling Mrs. Corrales as her man shakes hands with a father and son, a couple of young fight fans who had seen the Castillo fight. A fight the little boy describes as "the greatest fight ever!" and his father calls "the greatest ending to a fight that I've ever seen, we are both real big fans of yours." Mrs. Corrales just sits back smiling next to her man behind the podium, arms folded, looking radiant, as her husband beams obviously overwhelmed by the compliments, one can almost feel the pride drifting from her for her husband's accomplishments. What about the junior welterweight division? Would Diego take a rematch with Floyd Mayweather and potentially fight co-champion Ricky Hatton?

"Definitely, I would definitely fight Floyd again, I actually see that fight happening again, the last time I had a lot of outside pressures and things that helped influence that fight and I didn't have my mind on the fight then because of that" said Corrales "but I just don't see myself going up to junior welterweight and staying there anytime soon, if I fight Floyd again, it'll be somewhere else down the line, I'm really not too concerned about that fight right now."

Diego smiles to his wife as the next group of fans approaches the podium "that Castillo fight was just amazing! Can you sign this for my kid?" The champ looking like a kid with a hundred dollars in a candy store, obligingly signs for his newfound fans as his beautiful, wife looked on approvingly.

No, Diego Corrales doesn't have to worry about any potential rematches with either Mayweather or Castillo to define himself or his inevitable placement into the Hall of Fame, anymore. If he never fights again, give or take, fight fans both old and new will remember the night that he fought Jose Luis Castillo and pulled himself up from the dirge of defeat and showed the real-life heart that the average, mainstream fan only sees in the movies or on T.V… They saw the true, living, breathing heart of a champion.

POST-FIGHT:

Diego Corrales died on May 7th, 2007, exactly two years to the day of his epic battle with Jose Luis Castillo, on his new, 2007 Suzuki motorcycle in Las Vegas, he was apparently driving at a decent clip when he hit the back of a Honda Accord and was reportedly thrown almost the length of a football field, dying immediately upon impact…he was only 29 years old when he died. I feel very fortunate to have been given the opportunity by God to have met such a great individual and athlete and I can still remember his wide, bright, smiling face and I can only smile myself now…"Thank you, Diego, wherever you are…may God keep you in his immediate presence, forever and ever".

O'NEIL BELL INTERVIEW! PRE-FIGHT:

This interview contact was given to me, by my good buddy R.A. "The Rugged Man" and he introduced me to a man named Glenn Toby, a super nice gentleman who was managing a cruiserweight named O'Neil Bell. The cruiserweight division has always kind of been a lackluster division in boxing, sitting along the purgatory of light-heavyweight (175 pounds) and heavyweight (198 pounds and up), the cruiserweight division is traditionally a stopover point for light-heavyweights who're on their way to making better money for themselves in a heavier division, where they won't have to fight as frenetically against bigger guys, along with the added benefit of getting paid better, too. Cruiserweight fighters and even it's champions, are usually…at their very best…very placid fights to watch and even it's regular top-ten fighters at their worst…can be boring and lazy to watch for twelve rounds…creating a stinker. I took this interview to stay busy mostly, but I did know that it didn't take a whole lot for a fighter to become cruiserweight champion anymore and anyone with a big enough punch… could probably pick up at least one title. Not to say that Bell was talented…he is! I had seen Bell fight once before on TV and he appeared to have a big punch but, I thought he might be too mellow and fought a bit on the lethargic side, however, as I said before, it wouldn't take a whole lot to win a title at cruiserweight. Bell was a big guy for the weight class, he punched very hard and he'd already stopped most of the division's best fighters and resident tough guys and had aspirations of unifying the cruiserweight title like Evander Holyfield had done back in the 1980's. With all this in mind, (Bell had also knocked out Evander Holyfield's cousin in one of Bell's first couple of fights) I decided to take this interview…again, in story format written below, here are the results of that interview.

BOXING DIGEST INTERVIEWS... "CRUISERWEIGHT KING" O'NEIL "GIVE EM' HELL" BELL!

By
Richard Scurti

The cruiserweight division… has long been considered to be one of the most openly languishing weight classes in boxing since it's hey day in the late 1980's, when Evander Holyfield lit up the division after coming right out of the 1984 Olympics. Since then, fight fans have been thirsting for exciting fights to happen in a division that was seen largely by the public, as a stopping ground for overgrown light-heavyweights to make a little more money in a perpetually weak division. Boxing fans as a whole had just about given up on the hope that someone could come along and liven up the cruiserweight division in much the same way and manner that Evander Holyfield did over a decade before with his thrilling wins over Dwight Muhammad Quawi and Carlos DeLeon. Boxing fans had nearly lost all their hopes of finding another "Cruiserweight King" after the recent demise of potential "Cruiserweight King" Vasilli Jirov at the hands of James Toney last year. Yes, boxing fans have almost completely given up hope… that is… until now. Anyone who had seen the see-saw battle between "Lil Tyson" Kelvin Davis and O'Neil Bell can attest to the fact that we might have a new, potential, "Cruiserweight King" on our hands… O'Neil Bell. Bell, a fighter who, right after the Davis fight, would go on to knock out two top ten cruiserweights in Derrick Harmon in eight rounds and Ezra Sellers (a fighter who had also fought former heavyweight champion Bruce Seldon, getting knocked out in two rounds) also fell in two very short, rounds. Now, the thirty year-old, power-punching, knockout specialist, with 23 wins and (22 ko's) looks to become the best fighter in the cruiserweight division since the great, Evander Holyfield left it for the heavyweight division back in 1990. Bell, who is set to fight Dale Brown for the IBF cruiserweight title May 20th talked to Boxing Digest at length about the current state of the cruiserweight division, the greatness of Evander Holyfield (ironic for a man who's very first fight came against a fighter named Holyfield) and the possibility of Bell being the first man to unify the title for the first time in nearly twenty years. Bell, on the eve of his battle with "Cowboy" Dale Brown for the IBF cruiserweight championship of the world… now stands poised and ready to become the next "Cruiserweight King".

BD: O'Neill how does it feel to be fighting for the IBF cruiserweight championship of the world?

OB: It feels great! It's been a lifetime dream of mine to get to this point and I'll be in the best shape of my life for this fight. I want to win this one for myself, my father and for my
grandmother and most importantly; for my 6-year old daughter.

BD: Cool… How did you get started in boxing?
OB: I fought amateur first, I had twelve amateur fights went undefeated as an amateur. I was only twenty years old when I turned pro in 1996. I've been fighting for a long time and I just want my greatness to be recognized and I feel like I still haven't been recognized.

BD: Well' what would you say has been you toughest fight so far?

OB: I don't know… they all been so tough… I guess' Jose Rivera in St. Louis… it was tough as in… the atmosphere I was in was very hostile… but I went in there and knocked him out in eleven rounds and I still just rose above it. I try to separate myself from what goes on outside the ring and just kind of keep everything out there away from me and keep my mind on the fight... not on everything else.

BD: As a fighter with a record of 22-knockouts with 25 fights; do you feel that other boxers in your division are afraid to fight you? Meaning' what's up with the Kelvin Davis fight?

OB: Definitely, I've been the uncrowned champ in this division for well over six years! I've knocked out Ezra Sellers (a guy who fought former heavyweight champ Bruce Seldon), Derrick Harmon, Kelvin Davis and "King" Arthur Williams and I believe that I'm the greatest cruiserweight in the division right now and I know that I need to believe this without being too overconfident. Kelvin Davis doesn't want to fight me... he's scared to fight me. In the first fight, I clearly dominated him even though it was a rough and tough fight... I put him on the ropes. I would have liked to have faced him again in a rematch so that I could walk away as the obvious champ. But, he had no intention of really facing me again and I'll be looking forward to this fight with Dale Brown as a way to overcome that and become the world cruiserweight champion and current "Cruiserweight King".

BD: Speaking of "Cruiserweight Kings" do you feel that you can bring life back to the cruiserweight division in a manner to when the great, Evander Holyfield was there?

OB: I believe I do yeah'... Evander Holyfield was an incredible cruiserweight champion and an all-time great heavyweight champion, it would be an honor to follow in his footsteps and I know that I have the ability and talent to do so. I hope that I can have the opportunity to unify all three titles someday... but I know I must concentrate on beating Dale Brown and winning just one first. (laughs)

BD: Would you ever consider moving up to heavyweight?

OB: Definitely! I know that I can put that extra weight on eventually and fight at heavyweight as long as I can fight the very best out there.

That's always been my goal to fight the very best and right now I just want to concentrate on Dale Brown and be ready for a great fight with another great fighter.

BD: Besides Dale Brown is there anyone else out there that you would like to fight with?

OB: James Toney. I always want to fight the very best out there and right now James Toney is the very best fighter for me to fight, besides Dale Brown. I believe I have what it takes to fight another great fighter like James Toney and I believe that a fight with James Toney can bring that out of me.

BD: What do you see yourself doing before this next fight with Dale Brown?

OB: Just mainly, staying focused on fighting Brown for the IBF championship on May 20th. Fighters have been avoiding me for years, denying me my shot at glory, "I know Dale Brown is a true warrior and I know he will show up on May 20. I'm very excited to finally get my world title shot, and I'm going to make the most of this opportunity. I've been training very hard for this fight; lots of roadwork and sparring with Sherman "The Tank" Williams so that I can fight and be at my very best and be considered a great fighter.

BD: Great, is there anyway that your millions of fans can get in touch with you?

OB: Sure, they can go to www.oneilbell.com or go to my manager Glenn Toby's website www.glenntoby.com to see what's been going on with me. Pretty soon you'll be able to buy O'Neil's Gear Online on my website so that's currently in the works. The website is just going to get better and better as we add more stuff to it.

BD: Perfect, is there anything you want to say to your millions of fans out there, that read Boxing Digest?

Richard Scurti

OB: Just to hold tight, because I want to be a phenomenon in the making, I will capture that title! I'm currently number one with the fans and I plan on winning and then holding that title. My dream is to be to be the greatest champion to unify the cruiserweight title since the great, Evander Holyfield. I just want to say that I'm really thankful for all the support I've had ever since my amateur days in boxing till this very moment. I want to thank everyone…my mom and dad, my brothers, my manager Glenn Toby, for just getting me to where I am today.

POST-FIGHT:

O'Neil Bell did end up doing just what he said he would do...in unifying all three cruiserweight titles by knocking out Jean Marc Mormeck, the other belt holder, in a scorching fight...becoming the very first fighter to unify the cruiserweight division since the great Evander Holyfield. I got very lucky to have gotten this interview and I wish to thank R.A. and especially, Glenn Toby...for giving me the opportunity to interview his fighter, O'Neil Bell. Bell had recently fought a tough guy named Dale Brown right before this article came out and I had offered to write an interview with Bell with the intention of shedding a better light on the guy...I'm glad I did.

"SUGAR" RAY LEONARD INTERVIEW PART ONE OF THREE! PRE-FIGHT:

By
Richard Scurti

Another big one…that's the only thing I could think about, after interviewing Oscar De La Hoya and seeing it appear in a 2005 edition of Boxing Digest magazine. I got a lot of positive responses from people on the interview and all I could obsess on was doing an interview with another well-known boxer, one that most people would know. Ali, while extremely well know, was also very reclusive and not exactly in the greatest of health as of late and Oscar I had already interviewed. Around this time, ESPN had just started airing the second season of, "The Contender" a boxing reality TV show that I believe was originally shown on NBC, that was being hyped by both…Sylvester Stallone (we'll get to him, later) and… "Sugar" Ray Leonard. Also, during this time, I was hearing a rumor about how the Boxing Hall of Fame in Canostota, N.Y. was going to enshrine members of the 76' Olympic boxing team…which also included, "Sugar" Ray Leonard. Based on both of these things, I called my editor, Greg Juckett again and I got Ray's contact from him (sadly, this was one of the last times I spoke Greg, when he decided to leave the magazine not long after this interview was done, Greg was a great editor for the magazine and an even better friend to me, God Bless you, Greg). I contacted Ray and spoke with him for over an hour and I got enough of an interview with him to run the next three interviews within the pages of three different issues of Boxing Digest. These next three interviews were of course, written in story format, which actually made for an even better interview for most people to read. I hope you enjoy them…here are the results.

THE CHAMPION AND HIS "CONTENDERS"! THE LIFE AND TIMES OF SUGAR RAY LEONARD- PART-1!

By
Richard Scurti

This past month "Sugar" Ray Leonard talked exclusively with Boxing Digest writer Richard Scurti about his fights, his life, and his times as one of booing's, promoters and most recently, the creation of his highly acclaimed Sunday night boxing series on ESPN, "The Contender."

Seldom is the case a correct one, when a fighter takes on the surname of another famous fighter who fought before him. That fighter has to live up to the previous fighter's billing, his hype, his public image (being careful not to tarnish it) and eventually, his legend. "Sugar" Ray Leonard (named after Ray Charles) has more than earned that long sacred nickname of "Sugar" since he first streaked across the nations' television screens like a shooting star, during the 1976 Olympics. From out of the 76' Olympics that year, came six gold medal boxing winners, who coincidentally came at a time when America needed them most. The nation as a whole, was still reeling from the after effects of the Vietnam War and most Americans now, desperately needed something that they could believe in. America as a whole longed for a source of national pride that would make everyone feel good again, something that could help them to forget about the draining effects of war. The American public, hungry for a newfound sense of nationalistic pride, got behind the 76' Olympic boxing team like no other team before them. America in particular began to back a smooth, well spoken, young, boxer from Palmer Park, Maryland named "Sugar" Ray Leonard.

America had fallen in love with the colorful, articulate, bright, young man with the flashy hands and windswept movements in the ring, and the million-dollar-kilowatt smile he generated outside of it, when he defeated five amateur fighters that summer. America rejoiced with a surge of high nationalistic pride when he decisioned highly touted Cuban amateur champion Andres Aldama in the light-welterweight division, for a story book gold medal win in Montreal, Canada.

The bout was watched by most of America during mid afternoon on ABC Sports that day. Much the same way that Ray's highly acclaimed TV series "The Contender" would be watched by most of America every Sunday night on ESPN at 8:00pm nearly thirty years later (ironically, also during a period of war) and it was a bout that was fueled by the nationalism of the time.

"Aldama was the best all around fighter that I ever fought in the amateurs", recalled Ray "he was just knocking guys out, then! A lot of people thought that I couldn't beat him, my brother Roger said that I couldn't beat him! But I studied Aldama...I knew that he had that tall, stand up, rangy, style and I knew I could beat him just by moving in and out on him and flurrying during the last two minutes of every round...and I did."

Ray had fought through all his opponents with a picture of his girlfriend, Juanita taped to his boot. When no commercial endorsements came in after his Olympic win, Ray turned professional, taking on one top rated fighter after another in his newfound quest for the welterweight championship of the world.

"I did take a break after the Olympics and I kind of surveyed my options, now all of a sudden I had a girl and a kid to think about... boxing was something that I always did and wanted to do and I was good at it. So we put together a team of professional businessmen and I turned pro."

In 1977, Ray would defeat the more experienced Luis "The Bull" Vega and Willie "fireball" Rodriguez in only his first and second bouts, before taking on heavier and tougher competition. In 1978, Ray knocked out the original Floyd Mayweather, defeated former amateur star Randy Shields and stopped former NABF welterweight champion Armando Muniz inside of six rounds.

"Floyd Mayweather senior, fights just like the son does today; I can still see him leaning back on the ropes during our fight, in that awkward, defensive, crab-like shell. He was hard to hit and very crafty, but I eventually got to him, Floyd was an up and comer back then and I knew that. Floyd jr. on the other hand, is probably the most talented fighter there is today and he has said some things here and there about both me and my time period that I fought in. But, that's just all showbiz, Floyd is very cocky today and you need to be if you're going to get to be number one, besides...I was a little cocky myself back then."

The following year, he stopped cross town rival Johnny Gant in eight rounds, Fernand Mercotte, and floored Aldolfo Viruet- beating him easily in ten rounds (Viruet had previously gone the ten-round distance with Duran without hitting the canvas).

"Johnny Gant was such a big break for me, cause he was so well known in my area, people initially compared us... being from roughly the same area that it was a real pleasure to fight him, actually knocking him out was a big win for me and it really built my confidence up even more... in fact my brother Roger ended up beating him also." "Marcotte was also very tough and he was so strong that I think when I fought him he was actually weighing close to middleweight and actually, I believe he was the Canadian junior middleweight champion but I rocked him a few times and stopped him in the sixth."

Ray then knocked out in successive order, junior middleweight Tony Chiaverini in four rounds, Pete Ranzany also in four, and Andy Price in spectacular fashion in one round.

"Andy Price held wins over I think' both Pipino Cuevas and I think' Palomino too, so the knockout over him was very satisfying, I saw that Andy was hurt early and I stepped it up a notch and just finished him earlier than I really expected to. Before the fight, I knew who Andy Price was and I was a little nervous, but I knew in my heart that I would win, but I was still nervous because it was a big fight. Now, the day before the fight I arrived in Las Vegas and I went to see a friend of mine, Diana Ross's show and that she would be going to see a fighter on the same card as me that Marvin Gaye had, who was also fighting tomorrow night. "Oh' really!" exclaimed Diana "Marvin has a fighter that he manages!" I said "wow, what's the guys' name? Diana looked at me and said "Andy Price... do you happen to know him?" I said "Diana...that's the guy I'm going to be fighting tomorrow night." Diana looked at me and said, "well' don't hurt him too bad then."

Ray then took on, after that most impressive showing on ABC sports, the WBC welterweight champion, Wilfred Benitez. It was a classic game of cat and mouse, a chess game between two formally trained athletes, with both fighters trying to either outmaneuver or out think the other. For fifteen rounds Ray eventually just out slicked, outmaneuvered and even briefly floored the usually elusive Wilfred Benitez, before finally stopping a game, but outclassed Benitez in the final seconds of the fifteenth round.

"I take my hat off to him... he was just so hard to just... pin down and I was in the best shape of my life for that fight and I think that's what really made the difference. The fact that, whenever I do anything I always put one hundred and twenty percent of my effort behind it or into it and when I stopped Benitez in that last round, it was mainly because I had put all of my effort into finally stopping him. He hit hard in spots, more than a few times...mostly to the body though, Benitez was a game fighter and he would make you miss all night and if you didn't have that extra edge to continue fighting you would lose to him. Actually, the fight that I give a lot of credit to developing that kind of grit and stick-to-it-ness was the fight I had with Marcos Geralado. He just beat me around the ring for most of the fight; I mean he really put a beating on me! When I got into the ring with him, I looked across the ring at him and I realized that he was just so much more bigger than me! I mean, he was this six-foot tall Mexican guy who was really strong and real solid and man' he could fight! I stood my ground with him and planted my feet to really fight this guy and in reality, this guy was a middleweight! Somewhere during about the sixth round, I realized I would have to just dig down deep, find my heart and get into the trenches with this guy. So I really began to pour it on and landed the better more telling shots for the last four round and by the last round I think everyone could see that I was plainly hurting him by that point. That's why every fight I had after that one fight, I just wasn't afraid anymore. Because I figured that anything that anyone else could do to me, they couldn't be as tough or as strong or have beat on me as strongly as Geraldo did and I still dug down deep and came back from that to win a unanimous decision off of him. So by the time I was ready to face Duran, Benitez, or Tommy, I knew that I wouldn't be afraid of those guys and that nothing they could do would scare or hurt me."

"Today's fighters, have to learn from that as well, fighters are a unique breed of people who we either have what it takes to dig down deep in our soul and push on and come back or we can get stopped. But' even then, fighters today need to be able to learn from a loss or come back from a knockout and not stop. Some of my fighters who have fought on my TV show, The Contender really display those kinds of qualities.

I've seen the public really get behind a fighter or a young guy like Sergio Mora or especially Peter Manfredo Jr, everybody in America had just taken hold of that show. I notice that people really root for these guys much the same way that they did for me and my fellow teammates during the 76' Olympics, they begin to see the stories unfold on TV, the real-life behind the scenes stories that are actually being played out right in front of their eyes. Peter has just so much talent and I knew the public was really looking forward to seeing these two guys fight it out again at the Staples Center this past October.

We might eventually plan on bringing these guys out on a tour overseas due to the
enormous success of the show there. Where every couple of months these talented young men, can get a chance to showcase their talents to the whole world to see live. Of course everyone that watches the show and is big fans of our guys is just really hoping to tune into ESPN when the Contender will begin airing on Sundays at 8:00pm. People love seeing their favorite fighters dig down deep and try to come back. Why watch something unreal on TV, when you can follow the trials and tribulations of Peter Manfredo jr. or a hard luck story like Jeff Fraza's where he got sick with the chicken pox during the filming of the series. People have really felt for these guys after seeing what a fighter just goes through during the course of a day and people really began to just see themselves in these guys. It just really brings people back again and again to see the fights themselves and also what's going on in these great athletes' lives between their fights...people all over just can't get enough of what it's like to be a Contender."

"SUGAR" RAY LEONARD AND "THE CLASS OF 76'!"

By
Richard Scurti

When we watch Oscar De La Hoya and Floyd Mayweather fight multi-million dollar fights today, we tend to forget about the great fighters of the 1970s' period who helped bring them there. In the early seventies, many up and coming did just that...they fought. Many fighters fighting under heavyweight just fought each other in tough fights without any zest or flashy showmanship, if you weren't Ali, than flash didn't exist for the fans...there was nothing for the fans to get behind. It took an incredibly talented group of young amateur boxing stars during the 1976 Olympics, consisting of Leo Randolph, Davey Armstrong, Howard Davis jr., Leon and Michael Spinks, a patriotic, all-American team led by a young man, named "Sugar" Ray Leonard to change all that.

This past month Boxing Digest was granted another, exclusive, interview with "Sugar" Ray Leonard on his life and times during the Hall of Fame weekend in Canastota N.Y. Today, the Hall of Fame has brought together these great, former Olympians in an effort to say thank you from the bottom of America's hearts for the astounding patriotism they showed by winning gold medals for the United States... right when America needed them most. Today, Ray is the creator and host of "The Contender" the widely popular and highly aired boxing reality TV. show, currently airing on ESPN on Thursday nights.
Thirty years ago, out of the 76' Olympics and it's amateur program, came a wealth of phenomenal, fighters so stellar and spectacular, that it would take a new medium called pay-per-view, in order to properly display them to the American public. With fighters like Tommy Hearns, Howard Davis jr., "Sugar" Ray Leonard, Aaron Pryor, and Marvin Hagler, who were so good due to their amateur backgrounds,

that anyone from that late seventies period that were still around and still fighting under middleweight.... were instantly doomed.

When Tommy Hearns took out Eddie Gazo, Angel Espada, and finally Pipino Cuevas, and Leonard dusted Armando Muniz, Pete Ranzany, and Andy Price, it must have became painfully evident to the 70's welterweights... that their days were almost numbered. The junior-middleweight division then became something of a hiding spot, where for the moment, fighters like Tony Chiavareni, Eddie Gazo, Marcos Geraldo, Angel Espada, and many others could hide from facing the welterweights again by moving up in weight, without daring to move up to middleweight (because Marvin Hagler and Mustapha Hamsho were there).

Before this spectacular period, fighters just toiled away and strictly fought each other without much flair or spectacular talent, with the ambition mainly to just win a title for a little while and make some money (no one even thought of being close to the flash of Ali). Even previous stars of the seventies like Carlos Monzon and Emile Griffith didn't have the flash or style that some of these later fighters possessed.... fighting instead with a steady workman-like manner. Guys like Dave "Boy" Green, whom Ray Leonard fought after beating Benitez for the welterweight title... fought mainly just to make money. Nobody envisioned making millions for a single fight, not at the lower weight classes, that is until "Sugar" Ray Leonard came along.

"The defense against Dave "Boy" Green wasn't exactly the easy fight that people think it was", says Leonard with a smile "I had watched two of his really hard, tough, fights with Carlos Palomino and Andy Price, so I knew he was tough... there was no doubt about it. But, Angelo told me to "go out there and practice with Dave, left hooks, body shots and especially doubling up on them and that's what I did until I knocked him out." There's no hard feelings toward each other or anything, even today, I just had Dave over to my house not that long ago, we talk on the phone and we've been best friends ever since that fight. I think my knockouts of Dave Green, Tommy Hearns and Andy Price... are my three best knockouts of my whole career. The reason I handled Dave so easily was because of that amateur training that I had on my way to the 76' Olympics... a lot of people don't know that me, Davey Armstrong, Leo Randolph, Howard Davis jr., the Spinks brothers, were all together and learned from each other. Although, if I had to pick any one person as being my toughest fight for me all during my amateur days, I would have to say Bruce Curry. We fought each other like, three times and he was very tough to beat... every time out it was a tough fight, he could box and punch and he was also, the hardest puncher that I ever faced in the amateurs. Boxing with guys like Bruce Curry was never easy, but it really prepared me for what was to come."

After the Green fight, Sugar Ray Leonard's celebration was cut short when the newest, best, young fighter of the nineteen-eighties, took on the greatest fighter of the nineteen-seventies, the brutally, fearsome, Roberto Duran. Leonard then traveled back to Montreal, Canada, the site of his gold medal win to face Duran in the first Fight of the Decade fight on June 10, 1980.

Duran fought the fight of his life and was at his peak when he mauled and brawled with the very brave, but foolhardy Leonard, who tried to stand toe to toe with Duran, losing his welterweight championship in the process. "Duran did fight the fight of his life that night," said Leonard "it wasn't that I didn't know who Duran was or anything like that, but, he was much faster and craftier than people know in there. If there was one thing that I could say that made me lose that fight... it was Duran's body attack...by the end of the fight both of my sides were red and it was hard to raise my leg over the ring rope by the end of that fight. But I dug down deep and pulled out I think the last couple of rounds, even though I could hardly breathe by the end of the fifteenth round."

Leonard then after studying tapes of their first fight, came back and boxed beautifully against the onrushing Duran in their second fight. Leonard taunted Duran with bolo punches to his face, stinging him with flashy combinations and forcing Duran to utter the now famous words "no mas, no mas" (No More, No More,) in the eighth round.

Boxing's, Greatest Interviews!!

The referee called a halt to the fight with a tko for Leonard, while Duran no longer the bully that he once was...quit and walked away... complaining of stomach ailments.

"You know, he can say what he wants about that second fight (Duran), but he knows he was on his way to losing that one...he knew it and I knew it. I made him look like a fool inside the ring that night, in front of everyone and he knew the whole world was watching and he was very frustrated. He wasn't used to being treated so disrespectfully like that inside of a boxing ring and if there's one thing that I learned from Duran even before and definitely' during our first fight, it was that Duran is a man of honor and he lives for machismo. Later on, I watched how he tried to bull his way inside on me in our first fight and I was determined not to let him do it again. I knew I could outbox him now and to tell you the truth, towards the end of our second fight, I think he was afraid that he might get completely overwhelmed and even stopped by me."

But one still has to wonder...what about that bizarre outcome? "No Mas"? Not even Leonard could have predicted that one! "Honestly, I didn't even know what was going on at the end of that eighth round, I was hitting him to the body and then he just walked away from me. At first, I thought it might be a trick of Duran's or something, more head games from him. But then, I saw my corner and I saw Duran motion with his glove that he must not want to fight anymore and I knew that I had won the fight! Duran was a bully at the time and he lived off of that legend and when I clowned around with him and hit him with three bolo punches in the face, fast, pin-point punches, he was no longer scary and he was also embarrassed that he couldn't touch me. Plus, I was just beginning to work his body a little bit more and I think Duran felt like he was just now, becoming completely outclassed and that he might be on his way to getting knocked out by me."

Leonard than moved up to knockout junior middleweight champion; Ayule Kalule; before taking on the awesome, hard punching, WBA welterweight champion, Tommy "The Hitman" Hearns in a showdown of epic proportions (Hearns was 32-0 with 30 kayos before going into the fight).

"With Kalule, it was just business as usual really, I saw it as just another opportunity to stay sharp and pick up another title in a different weight class. I had watched tapes of Kalule and I saw that he was strong, but not very mobile and I stopped him pretty easily. This was also during the time that we began negotiations for the fight with Tommy and I knew that if I was going to fight Tommy, Kalule would be a big step forward."

Also during this time, Aaron Pryor came storming out of no where as the junior welterweight champion and everyone salivated over the thought of Leonard/Pryor...two former amateur stars who knew of each other, Fire vs. Ice! A dream match-up if there ever was one! You have to ask... why that fight never took place at any point during Leonard's early career or before his first retirement?

"I don't know why that fight never came off? That's a good question, because that would have been great... I know Mike Trainer was working hard at putting that one together at one point. We knew each other from our amateur days and Aaron used to come down to Palmer Park, Maryland and stay with me and my family for months at a time as a sparring partner. He was always a good friend but, it's too bad that fight never came off, we became friends all the way from the 76' Olympics until today. I actually did the intro to Aaron's book "Flight of the Hawk" but, he had his own problems to deal with... that might've made it hard for that fight to come off. Any truth to the rumor than, that you were scared to fight Pryor in the amateurs at lightweight and jumped up a weight class to junior welterweight or that Aaron had knocked you down in sparring?

"No, I was always a fighter, I loved it and I was very good at it naturally, so I was never afraid to fight anyone. At that particular time, my body just grew and junior welterweight was as light as my body could get at that time. Plus, I think there was a berth open at that weight class going into the Olympics, so I just concentrated on that weight class. As for knocking me down in sparring, no' never happened, every sparring session with Aaron was a fight. But I was never worried, I would have beaten him as an amateur or a pro, but that's also something I think we both have our own opinions on", laughed Leonard.

Ray was no longer laughing when he signed on to fight Tommy "The Hitman" Hearns...he was serious. He had to be, like the guys from "The Contender" series that Ray now hosts on ESPN, Ray knew there was no room for error this time...no room for even a tiny mistake with Tommy Hearns. A fighter who had a reach equal to that of Muhammad Ali's and fearsome dynamite in his right hand, that left guys like Pipino Cuevas knocked senseless, down on the floor in less than two rounds and sporting a nasty left hook to the body to boot... Ray knew that against Tommy, you can either get serious or you can just pack your bags up and go home.

"Again, I hate to say this, but I knew who Tommy was from the 76' Olympics and our amateur days", laughed Leonard "I didn't actually fight Tommy in the amateurs, he was a weight class under me however, I did see him fight Aaron Pryor in the amateurs, so I was familiar with his style. But, people really don't know that, Tommy from the amateurs wasn't the Tommy of the pro's...he hit much, much harder later on in the pros. During our first fight, he didn't really catch me with too much and I think he was more concerned with out boxing me. Early on he wanted to make it a fight and I just wouldn't let him do it. But, to tell you the truth, the punch that did it was a left hook to Tommy's side in one of the middle rounds and he winced and dropped his guard and after that I knew I had him."

But what about that famous bit of wisdom given to Ray by Angelo Dundee "You're blow' in it son, yer' blow' in it!" did Ray really have it all in the bag even then? Could that fight have ended the same way Trinidad/De la Hoya did?

"I thought that I was ahead on the cards at the time of the eleventh round and I knew that Tommy was definitely hurt, but Angelo did wake me up with that saying. After that point, I took a deep breath and just really powered right through Tommy, who was too tired and spent. As far as Trinidad/De la Hoya goes, I don't think there would ever be that much inaction in any of our fights in the eighties. We all knew we were getting paid millions of dollars to fight each other too, but in the end, we still wanted to know, "who's the very best of us" whether it was me and Tommy or Tommy and Marvin, Duran and me, it didn't matter. We wanted bragging rights above all else, kind of like the way that rappers today have "battles" we wanted to see "who was the man."

On that note, you have to wonder how fighters like Ray see today's fighters like Oscar De la Hoya or Felix Trinidad?

"There are some very good fighters out there today, but not a whole lot. That's one of the reasons that I put out "the Contender" to give more fighters who have working class lives, a chance to get the exposure that they normally would never have... worldwide. Kids from all over the whole, wide, world come up and they know Sergio Mora and Alfonso Gomez, they know them, the way that you and I would know... Muhammad Ali. It's a great show and I'm glad it's getting the great ratings that it's been getting. Today, aside from Oscar and Floyd... there isn't too many extremely, talented, fighters out there today, not like there was during the early eighties. It's funny... you ask how would Oscar or Tito Trinidad do during my time period? I've seen them both fight and all I can say is they're very good fighters, maybe even great. But, could you really see Tito Trinidad in there against six foot-one, Tommy Hearns, who's going to put that laser-like jab in his face all night and then follow it up with his right hand? I mean, come on Richard'... you know you can't see Oscar in there with Tommy either. Tommy had it all and believe me I know... it took me almost an entire fight to beat him!"

Leonard stopped Tommy Hearns in fourteen rounds, in a classic match-up of two ring immortals, meeting each other within their respective primes, before retiring briefly.

SUGAR RAY LEONARD-PART-III
THE CHAMPION RETIRES...
"THE CONTENDER" IS BORN"

By Richard Scurti

Sugar Ray Leonard spoke candidly again, with Boxing Digest correspondent Richard Scurti, about the moments immediately following the 1st Leonard-Hearns fight and his subsequent fights after that. Along with his biggest wins, his greatest triumphs; including his win over Marvelous Marvin Hagler and the creation of his highly acclaimed television series, "The Contender" currently airing on both ESPN and ESPN-2.

"The first fight with Tommy Hearns was hard and he detached my retina with a right hand that was already slightly damaged from the Geraldo fight, that Tommy kind of grazed my eye in that fight first is what made me slow things down a bit. But when you ask me a question about that fight and how hard Tommy punched, he really didn't tag me with much during the first fight. But he did hit me a lot harder in our second fight... I think Tommy was a lot stronger for the second fight because he was at a higher weight class. It didn't matter too much though, I felt I did edge him at the end of the fight, but if they gave the fight to Tommy, I would have understood because he did put up a tremendous effort, but I powered through him at the end again and Tommy was holding on to keep from being knocked out and I think that's why they gave it to me."

Ray smiles, "Yes and no...most people don't know that there was no fight to be made at that time, I was retiring anyway and I guess Marvin and the Petronelli's were there to kind of show who was in charge. I just let them know right off of the bat that, they weren't in charge, I never waited for Marvin to retire or anything, that's ridiculous, bulls$@t... but, I did want any potential fight with Marvin to go by my rules. So, they were there and I made that announcement and if it got to Marvin than...so be it and I definitely knew that fight would someday happen...I just didn't know when it was going to happen."

Then, in 1987, Ray came out of a four-year retirement to take on the undisputed middleweight champion "Marvelous" Marvin Hagler. Leonard was absolutely positive he had the "perfect" plan to defeat "The Marvelous One" and then proceeded to beat Hagler to the punch, flurrying and moving on the undisputed champion, even stopping him in his tracks with fast one-two combinations. Leonard took Hagler's title in twelve rounds in a "perfect fight plan" before then relinquishing his belts and quickly retiring again.

"I did have the perfect fight plan, but a lot of it was also mind games with Marvin, to really, put in an effort to get Marvin to even think that he could lose, that was also part of the plan. You see, Marvin never really believed that he could lose, he was the undisputed middleweight champion for years and I really was trying to get him to even just believe in the possibility of him losing those belts. I knew that I was going to win when... we were at the press conference for our fight in Las Vegas and Marvin said to a reporter who had asked him if he would retire if he lost, he started off by saying that "he would retire and never fight again if the powers that be, tried to take his crown from him" I looked over and I thought, "I got this sucker now!" He knows that he lost that fight, Marvin knows it and I know it! He didn't want a "real" rematch that's why he invented this whole idea that the powers that be took his belts. I told him on an HBO broadcast that he lost and if he wanted to fight again I was more than willing...Marvin didn't want it because he was afraid he'd lose bigger maybe, the second time around...maybe where he was knocked out. If Marvin was aware of anything, it was his legend and his place in history and he didn't want to tarnish that and Marvin was bitter, but he rode off into the sunset. We've only just become friends within the past couple of years where we could finally talk together and pose for pictures."

Leonard then beat light-heavyweight champion Donny Lalonde for the WBC super middleweight and light-heavyweight titles, fought a draw with Tommy Hearns (which many people gave to Tommy) and beat Roberto Duran in their rubber match and with his fight goals now complete Leonard retired once again.

Ray sighs, "First off, Donny Lalonde hit the hardest out of everybody… and that includes Tommy Hearns… who would rank 2nd in our second fight. Donny was a big, strong kid and his punch was pulverizing… like a sledgehammer…I was very happy when it ended! Tommy also hit almost as hard in our second fight, he caught me up behind the head and I thought that he had dropped me and that I wouldn't get back up, my legs felt rubbery, but I did get up and continue. I think that's when my leg was just beginning to become bad after hitting the canvas twice against Tommy, that might have contributed to my third fight with Duran being as stale as the fight was, my leg hurt for the third Duran fight and I could feel it even then. After beating Duran, I was ready to stay retired by that point and stay behind the broadcast booth, I felt like I might have had enough."

He did unfortunately return twice to be beaten badly by Terry Norris and was Knocked out by Hector Camacho in 1997. He then worked behind the scenes promoting his own fights around the country and on ESPN-2.

You know, as soon as I got into the ring with Terry Norris…I knew it was going to be a bad night…he beat me cleanly and badly too… I might add and I should have just quit. But I couldn't stay away… it was just my ego really, telling me to keep going and keep competing. I should never have lost to Camacho though, that wasn't just my ego driving me, but my body really was hurt. My leg was shot up with Novocain and painkillers, I was really hurting. I still lost because, I just got old and I didn't believe it. It was just so hard to believe that there were new stars in boxing around my old weight class like; Pernell Whitaker and Chavez and Roy Jones."

Be that as it may, how hard was it to swallow seeing guys like Whitaker and Jones making it as latest boxing star, how does Ray see them as fighters? Is "The Contender" just a natural progression than, of no real big boxing stars on TV. like there was on ABC and NBC during the early eighties?

Pernell Whitaker, is without a doubt one of the greatest lightweight champs of all time! Without a doubt, the greatest defensive fighter of all time, if he didn't want you to touch him you didn't! I don't think he'd have beaten Duran or anything…I mean, we probably didn't see "Pete's" personal best at any point during his whole career and it would have taken Duran or somebody else like him, to push "Pete" to his limits. But unfortunately, he never really had that kind of competition that could drive him to further his goals. Same thing with Roy Jones to a degree, Roy did have some people that he could have fought against… but didn't… and that's what he'll probably be most remembered for. I'm real good friends with Pernell we talk on the phone quite a bit and we got to meet up together at the Hall of Fame this year and it's always a pleasure to speak with him. Pernell could have fought and beat every one of the lightweights from our era, except Duran and maybe, Camacho…that would have been a good fight. Roy Jones I've also met and seen fight a number of times and you ask… could he have fought in our era, it's difficult to say…he's bigger than everybody but Tommy and you can see now that in his last couple of fights that he could be knocked out. However, everybody has their off nights and Roy…probably would have been competitive during our period, but it's too hard to tell to what degree he'd have been.

"I'm so glad to be doing "The Contender", after my last promotional reign, that was just bad business decisions back then and I was just doing things with the wrong partner. The Contender" itself, is very much like when Wide World of Sports was on TV. back in the eighties, the show revolves around the type of guys today who are mostly working class with young families…and no connections! Their stories remind people of their own stories and being down on their luck and what it's like to struggle against the odds and win! People always come over to me and tell me how they know these fighters stories so well and how, they like them all so much, that they root not just for guys like Sergio Mora and Alfonso Gomez themselves…but they're rooting for their families as well! Everyone wants to see the underdog win and that's what this show has really capitalized on, this show has just grown to be so big here in America… that we're planning on bringing the show overseas to both Europe and Japan. Why watch something made up and unreal on TV. every week, following the same tired scripts…. when you can watch the real-life drama of a man battling against the odds to make his dream come true and become "The Contender's-Champion"…that's what makes this show and the lives it revolves around interesting and definitely, worth watching every week."

POST-FIGHT:

"The Contender" would go on to become one of ESPN's highest ranking shows that season and I feel very appreciative of Ray Leonard's generosity to give me the opportunity for this big, long interview… thanks, Ray! Now every time that I see you on Jay Leno or Carson Daly I can sit back in bed with my wife and smile, God blessed me that day. Ray Leonard has been and always will be bigger than boxing and larger than life, with Ray…who's involved in everything…there really is no post-fight commentary…only current commentary.

BUDDY MCGIRT
INTERVIEW
PRE-FIGHT:

This interview actually came from a publicist friend of mine who dealt mostly with rappers (you'll actually have to read my next book to read about what the world's greatest rap artists have to say about boxing, come on' you didn't think I _wouldn't_ be plugging my next book within these pages, now did you?) who also happen to be the publicist for Buddy McGirt. Buddy was a former fighter who held both the welterweight and jr. welterweight championships in the late 1980's and early 1990's, before becoming an even more stellar boxing trainer, by the late 1990's. Buddy would become most famous, thus far, for his resurrecting former jr. lightweight titleholder, Arturo Gatti, (teaching him how to box instead of slug) when most everyone else in the boxing world, had given up on Gatti…Buddy would become "Trainer of the Year" in 2003, when Gatti would win his second world title at jr. welterweight. I spoke with Buddy for about twenty minutes and these are the results…I hope that you all like them.

BOXING DIGEST INTERVIEWS... JAMES "BUDDY" MCGIRT!

By
Richard Scurti

BD: How are things going out there?
BM: Really good...I can't complain, as of right now I'm getting ready for my son Buddy's fight. He's going to be fighting Aaron Pryor's son in Michigan, so I'm pretty excited, Buddy's going to win that fight easily...we plan to stick and move and box him a little bit.

BD: Being that we're on the eve of your son's fight with Aaron jr.... a lot of people would probably want to know how you think that you've done against Aaron Pryor sr.?
BM: As a fighter, I would like to say that I would've beaten him... I looked up to Aaron when I was on my way up and I think it would have been a hell of a fight. When I first started boxing, I bought a t-shirt shirt that said "What time is it? Aaron Pryor training camp" at the Ohio state fair and I used to just wear that shirt everywhere and I'd work out in it thinking about the day when I'd fight him." But you never know? I think it would've been a great fight though.

BD: Are you going to be in Arturo Gatti's corner in the upcoming Gatti/Baldomir fight? If Gatti wins...what do you see him doing and if he loses?
BM: Yes, I'll still be in Arturo's corner for as long as he asks me to, I'll be working his corner for the Baldomir fight. If he wins, I think that he'll still think about what he wants to do even if he were to win or lose this fight. Arturo has family and his health to think about and it's his call either way now, at his age whether he wins or loses doesn't matter, it's how much longer he feels like doing it. It's not really a win or lose situation for him anymore, it's whether he wants to keep doing it now.

Of course, I'll have a say in it and I've always been honest with Arturo, but ultimately it's his decision, whether he decides to continue or not. If he decides to go on, win or lose, I'll continue to be in his corner, every step of the way and we'll then make the proper adjustments.

BD: What do you see Gatti's chances against Baldomir being? How do you see him doing after the Mayweather fight?
BM: Arturo's chances are always good I don't know, it depends, Baldomir is a strong, guy and Arturo can punch with him but, I'm going to probably ask that he takes his time and work on him. But you never know? Against Floyd, Arturo didn't have to take that fight… he wanted to take that fight. We all felt that is was the right fight at the right time and win or lose it was going to' be a real good fight, no question about it. Floyd's probably the best fighter in the world right now and we knew that but, there were things that we all saw in his fights and his training that we felt we could exploit….we tried and that's all there is to it.

BD: So, you felt that Arturo had a puncher's chance with him? What were your reasons for stopping the fight when you did?
BM: Not just a puncher's chance, Arturo had a fighter's chance of beating Floyd, I knew it was going to' be a hard fight, Arturo knew it was going to' be a hard fight. But Arturo has a style that, on his best night could've presented real problems for Floyd and that's what we were banking on. We all had a say in stopping that fight…even Arturo had a say in it when he came back to me in the next to last round he said, "Coach, I can't see him," Arturo had a say as well. My reasons for stopping the fight when I did was, I could look at his face the round before I stopped it and I could see in his face, the chances were becoming less and less and rather than risk any eye damage for my fighter, I finally just said, "that's it baby, they'll be other fights, I'm going to' stop it". It was the right decision to make, as a trainer, he's my fighter to take care of and I'm supposed to look out for his best interests and I think I said it correctly, "they'll be other fights."

BD: What about a fight with Ricky Hatton, do you think Arturo could beat him?

BM: That's not really for me to decide, that's up to both, Arturo and Pat Lynch as well as his promoter to decide. But, you know, if you're asking me if he could beat Ricky Hatton, yeah' I would expect him to, Arturo could take him and it'd be a hell of a fight. But that's a fight that I don't think will happen for a lot of different reasons, but mostly because their basic promotions would hold that up and probably keep it from happening.

BD: You've also been in the corners of many other great fighters as well, who was the best or most talented that you handled?
BM: I'm sorry, I can't really say that' hoss. They're all real talented I couldn't really say that anybody was the most talented, I just, I don't say those things about my fighters, they're all great fighters in my book, I'm sorry' but I really can't comment on that."

BD: Not a problem, you were in Antonio Tarver's corner in his last couple of fights, where he lost his title twice? He's been accused of being kind of a lazy fighter in the past…do you think that, coupled with him starring in the latest "Rocky Balboa" movie, contributed to his downfall?
BM: No, not at all, Antonio loses interest sometimes during the fight, but not during training and as a trainer, you kind of have to try to help bring it back to him again during the fight and other times it's up to the fighter himself, it depends, you know. There's stuff that happens both in and out of the ring that you're dealing with and Antonio came off of the two wins over Roy Jones. So, he might've been riding that high a little, I don't know…I've worked with Antonio for a few years now and I'm going to keep working with him, he's a real good guy and he's easy to train.

BD: Do you think that he might have been riding that "high" as you call it, when Roy Jones was knocked out by Antonio…I mean, we all know that Roy Jones was a 'target" of Antonio's after they had fought as amateurs and Antonio beat him then…do you think Antonio played the part of Rodrigo Valdez to Jones' Carlos Monzon? Where we saw the best of Tarver because there was Roy Jones for him to play off of?

BM: No, not really, I can tell you first hand that, Antonio was a fighter' long before there ever was Roy Jones, did he become more focused because Roy was there yeah, probably but, I think Antonio fought as good a fight against Roy Jones as he did against Glen Johnson right afterwards when he lost to Glen and then beat him. Antonio comes to fight, right now, I don't think he cares whether it's Roy or anybody else standing in the ring across from him, Roy was just one more mountain for him to climb, that's all."

BD: What about Lamon Brewster, he just lost his title recently…do you think he lost his focus?
BM: Lamon is a good fighter and I think he might need to refocus himself a little bit, yeah' he put forth a good effort against Lyakhovich but, not the great one needed to beat this guy…Serguei came to fight and I tried to implore him to pick up the pace a little bit…but it just wasn't enough…Lamon put him down, but Serguei, just wanted it more, that's all. So yeah' I think Lamon's going to be talking with his family and stuff and he'll probably have to reassess where and what he wants to do now. As far as his future fights goes, I'll continue to work with Lamon as well as the other fighters I've always worked with.

BD: As a fighter you fought many greats over the length of your boxing career? Who was your toughest fight?
BM: A lot of people when they meet me for the first time and they ask me that question, they seem to think that I'm going to say Pernell Whitaker was my toughest fights… but he wasn't! The toughest fight of my whole career was the first fight with Frankie Warren, he beat the crap out of me and he was much tougher than I expected him to be.

BD: What about the hardest puncher you ever faced?
BM: Two people, probably Simon Brown was the overall hardest puncher I ever faced he hit me real, real, hard and he was beating me for much of the fight I thought, until I put him on the floor in the tenth round, I think' that won the fight and Tony Baltazar, he hit me very hard too, even though I was off balance a little bit.

BD: What about "The Outlaw" Jesse James Hughes...you fought him too...do you remember him?
BM: Oh yeah, we fought in Ft. Lauderdale, it was very hot that day and I sweated a lot even before the bout actually even started. Yeah' I remember him, he was really strong and he was in top condition and I'll never forget how this guy just kept coming at me. That was the kind of incredible, physical shape that this guy was in, he just forced and pushed his way through you; he was physically unstoppable and I just out boxed him.

BD: Was he a hard puncher?
BM: Yeah' but not like you think, he was kind of a clubber, he just clubbed you to death, right on top of you all the time and I just remember how strong he was and how relentless he fought...I was glad when the fight finally ended.

BD: What about "Pete", Pernell Whitaker, your two fights with him were classics...what are your thoughts on him and those two fights in particular?
BM: "Pete" I would say is one of the greatest defensive fighters of all time...I wouldn't necessarily say that he's an all-time great all around fighter, though. When we fought, I put him down and that was never an easy thing to do, although, at lightweight I would have to rate him pretty high though. But no' I have no bad feelings toward Pete' he was a great champion and today, I just think that we both fought in a couple of real good fights. He wasn't my toughest fight, but he was just a real hard guy to figure out once you were inside of the ring with him.

BD: What's in the future for Buddy McGirt as a trainer and as a person?
BM: I'll continue to train my son Buddy jr. he has a great future ahead of him, I'll continue to work with Arturo and Lamon, I'll be there for Antonio as well, you know? I'm just happy to be here and I feel really... just, blessed from God, you know? I overcame injuries to my body, financial difficulties and bankruptcy... to be here all over again...I just feel very, very, blessed. I was just in Irvington, NJ where I got to speak with underprivileged children in Irvington as well as

Jersey City this past summer, if my story can give these kids hope and give them a chance to get ahead, I'm all for it. I'll be available to speak at the schools and let kids know about the dangers of gang violence and to be able to kind of preach anti-violence is a really beautiful thing to be a part of and I'm really all for that kind of stuff. Like I said, I feel blessed by God and I'm going to do as much as I can to let people know that, when you go looking to find it...God will give you that second chance.

POST-FIGHT:

After this interview was done, Buddy would go on to work with other world champions such as light-heavyweight and heavyweight champions; Antonio Tarver, Lamon Brewster, among many others. Because of his success with Arturo Gatti, Buddy continues to be in high demand by fighters worldwide and can often be seen today working the corners of fighters on HBO and Showtime networks. I felt honored to have had the distinct opportunity to interview Buddy and I personally feel like this is one of my most inspirational interviews, I thank God for this opportunity and Buddy for giving me the time in his busy schedule to speak with me.

<u>KEN BUCHANAN INTERVIEW PRE-FIGHT:</u>

This interview came about at the 2006 Boxing Hall of Fame, I was walking about one of the restaurants during Hall of Fame weekend, when who should I run into but, former lightweight champion, Ken Buchanan! Ken, became the lightweight champion of the world during the early 1970's by beating all-time great champion, Panamanian, Ismael Laguna, twice. Laguna at that time, was considered nearly unbeatable and everyone thought he'd be "the man to beat" for years to come…until Ken beat him for Laguna's lightweight title. Ken had only fought twice before defending his lightweight title against unknown, all-time great, Roberto Duran (to give non-boxing fans an idea of how tough fighting Duran was at this time, it would be like fighting Mike Tyson before he was champion and became famous or playing Michael Jordan before he was with the Chicago Bulls…*in short, Ken had no idea how good Duran really was or how great he would become years later)*. This interview, in story format, was designed to let everyone know how great of a champion that Ken Buchanan really was…I'd be very happy if you feel the same way after you read this interview.

THE CROWNING MOMENT OF... KEN BUCHANAN!

By
Richard Scurti

Sometimes when we think of crowning moments within the sport of boxing, as boxing fans, we tend to think of when, great fighters either win or defend their titles in great fights. But sometimes, the real great test, the real great testament to a fighters' ability, can come in tough fights that they barely win or can barely withstand, in either the beginning or ending of their careers. Such was the case when Ken Buchanan was set to defend his lightweight title in Madison Square Garden on June, 26th 1972, against an unknown fighter as a late last-minute substitute, when Ken's original opponent dropped out of the title match, only days before the actual fight was to take place. Ken, completely confident in his ability as one of Europe's best young fighters at the time, had no qualms at all with defending the championship crown on such short notice...against whoever that may be. Because that's what a "fighting champion" does... he fights... against all comers, even when he doesn't have to or he shouldn't have to fight. Then it must have been a combination of both fate and Ken's incredible courage that made him take that fight, during that hot, summer night back in 1972, when he didn't have to fight at all and did, against a very, young, legend in the making, named... Roberto Duran. This is Ken's account of that night and the events that led up to a crowning moment for not one, but two all-time great fighters, when they both crossed paths during the New York City heat wave of 1972, at Madison Square Garden.

RS: Ken, you're a former lightweight champ from the nineteen seventies and you've fought everybody from Carlos Ortiz to Ismael Laguna to Jim Watt and Roberto Duran. What's your take on someone like Ricky Hatton who's tried to move up in weight recently, good for Ricky or not good?

KB: Not good! You can see that he wanted that other title in another weight class but, it's my opinion that he just should not stay there! He's a good enough banger at a lower weight but, you could really see that in that Callazzo fight, he would hit the guy with his Sunday punch and the guy's still there and could take it! So no' he should definitely stay down in weight again, if I were him I'd just drop the belt and stay at junior welterweight.

RS: As far as your part in boxing history, as a lightweight champion, you're kind of like a common denominator, being that you fought Ortiz, Laguna, Watt and Duran…out of those four guys who was the best…

KB: Duran! Without a doubt! He was just awesome in there! Just awesome! He was on me from the first round on and he just smothered me in there…I couldn't breathe! Everywhere I turned that night and he was on me like a f^*^$ing octopus! Without a doubt he was the best of all of them and I can personally tell you that, the other three guys weren't even in Duran's league! He moved at a much faster speed and pace than they ever did, none of the other three guys you mentioned could have stayed in there with him… not on that night!

RS: Out of everybody you fought both champions and contenders who hit you the hardest? You have Guts Suzuki, Jim Watt who had a good right hand, Ortiz…

KB: Duran! Hands down! He dropped me early in the first round with a straight right hand and I just, never saw it coming! Every punch hurt really bad and he was just an awesomely hard hitter with either hand, he bulled into me with his head and followed it up with a straight right every time in that fight and it took everything I had to stay upright by the end of that fight…every time he hit me in the face…my teeth ached.

RS: Wow, you're kidding? Why didn't you train harder if you knew you were going up against Duran?

KB: Who the f$^& was Duran? I didn't know! Listen, I was supposed to defend my title against somebody else that night, I can't remember what the guys' name was or anything, but the guy fell out of the fight due to an injury or something. So a couple days before the fight, the promoter comes up to me and says he has a replacement for me. He says he has this guy who had just fought at MSG and knocked out his opponent in one round and is still in New York for me to fight. I'm confident as hell and I said, "Fine, who is he?" and the promoter says, "Roberto Duran" and I'm like, "fine bring him on, then." To which my manager, Gil Clancy and my trainer both turn and look at me and say, "Now, are you sure you're ready for Duran?" and I looked at them both and said, "Sure, who the f%&* is Duran?" I had no idea who he was or who he was going to end up being, I really didn't… until it was too late and the night of the fight! When, it took everything for me to stay in there with him.

RS: Wow, so that was kind of like, you're a heavyweight champion and you're getting ready to defend your title and the guy you trained for is replaced by a young, up and coming Joe Louis and no one's even aware of who he is yet?
KB: Exactly! I had no idea I was going to end up fighting one of the greatest lightweight champions of all time! I used to train by running four to five miles a day and I wouldn't have lasted like I did until that ending if it weren't for that training and that's all I'll say about that! (Ken makes a motion with his hand that the interview is over.)

RS: Great, thank you for your time, Ken…you're an all-time great champion in my book.
KB: Thank you, Rick…it's always a pleasure for me to speak with my fans.

Ken Buchanan lost his lightweight title that night to the great Roberto Duran…which would become the first of many such titles for Duran, a fighter who would later go on to annex world championships in a record four weight classes, becoming the first Latino fighter to ever accomplish the feat. For Ken Buchanan, a fighter who's final record, stood at 61 wins, 8 losses, (five of which happened after the Duran fight, a fight which was so brutally horrid for Ken to have engaged in, that the physical effects of the fight, clearly forced him past his prime) and with half of those wins coming by way of knockout (27 ko's). It then becomes clear that Ken Buchanan was no ordinary fighter, for no ordinary fighter could have withstood the extraordinary amount of punishment he endured in his last-minute fight with a substitute, Roberto Duran. The Duran fight was a crowning moment for Ken (as no one else could have lasted that long with the future great, Duran then, only just a legend in the making), where… he may have lost a title…but none of his dignity. After winning his lightweight title from Panamanian Ismael Laguna, during two hard fought, fifteen round fights, it's only fitting then that he would relinquish it to another Panamanian great, in Roberto Duran. Ken Buchanan would go on to later defeat future hall of famer, Carlos Ortiz (tko-6) and future lightweight champion, Jim Watt by decision over fifteen rounds. Ken Buchanan can feel eternally proud for accomplishing yet another great, crowning moment, on top of so many other great moments that he had during his entire boxing career. By just staying in there the way that he did with Duran back in 1972, one wouldn't have expected any more from him, but that's what it was for Ken Buchanan, a "fighting champion" if ever there ever was one. By lasting the distance that he did, against the legendary opponent sprung onto him by fate… to have stayed in there when every other champion of the time would have fallen, for Ken Buchanan… it was just one more crowning moment, for him… it was just another, great, accomplishment.

POST-FIGHT:

Ken Buchanan is an all-time great boxing champion who was voted into the Boxing Hall of Fame, every year just about Ken comes to the Hall and was at Roberto Duran's induction in 2007. he spoke with Duran Jokingly and they both posed for pictures together, proving that even in boxing, former enemies, can often become lasting friends, later on in life.

SYLVESTER STALLONE INTERVIEW PRE-FIGHT:

This was in many ways, the biggest interview of them all...because of this man and the movie that he wrote back in 1976, I became a boxing fan, in November of 2006, I was fortunate enough to have interviewed Sylvester Stallone. First, I have to thank Ray Leonard for his first telling Sly and his publicist about me, after I had interviewed Ray, back in 2005. I had been trying for about a year since then, to get an interview with Sly, to little to no avail. Around that time, "The Contender" reality TV show, was in full force and was still going strong when I had heard and read that Sly would be doing another, "Rocky" and another, "Rambo" after that film. I thought "perfect" the timing for this interview would be "perfect", if I could just get an interview with Sly. So, I called Sly's publicist in L.A. up and asked for her...completely cold. Somehow, this time...I got through to her and somehow talked her into letting me interview him. So, after much back and forth between my new editor at Boxing Digest magazine, Sean Sullivan and (Sean had come onto the magazine after my former editor and friend, Greg Juckett had left) Sly's publicist...we had struck a deal and I was given a time to interview Sly on November 16, 2006... wow! I was star struck! The only thing was, in order to get the interview into the latest issue before the, "Rocky" movie came out in late December, I had to type it up and e-mail it in less than an hour after interviewing Sly...*talk about pressure!* I felt that I could do it and told them both, "yes" even though, I had no idea how I was going to do it. Anyway, November 16th 2006 finally came and I was ready, below is the results of my interview with "Rocky" aka. Sylvester Stallone.

"THE UNDERDOG ROCKY BALBOA'S BACK ON TOP!" SLY STALLONE SPEAKS... AND YOU WON'T BELIEVE ALL THAT HE HAS TO SAY!

Interview
by Richard Scurti

This past month, Boxing Digest staff writer got to speak to the man who created the most iconic character in the sport of boxing, "Rocky Balboa". In 1976, the world was at war and America was in need of something to boost their hopes up. Americans got it in the form of a come from behind movie about a down and out club fighter from Philadelphia, Pa, who is given a once in a lifetime opportunity to fight for the heavyweight championship of the world, against the Muhammad Ali-like character of Apollo Creed…in the process gaining respect not for winning the title…but going the full 15-round distance with the heavyweight champion of the world. Now, in 2006, Americans will once again get the chance to experience those feeling of "rooting for the underdog", when Sly Stallone's, "Rocky Balboa" hits theatres Dec. 22nd nationwide. Americans will finally get a chance to see a national, American institution, for the first time in over fifteen years since the last "Rocky" came out. As usual, Sly plans to follow-up on the immediate success of "Rocky Balboa" with "Rambo-4" and an even more interesting movie piece on the life of Edgar Allan Poe. Today, we got to talk to the man most responsible for America's interest and resurgence in boxing when he released the original "Rocky" in 1976 and how it feels to be able to do it all again this December 22nd, 2006.

After fifteen years since the last "Rocky" do we get to see the improbable happen in, "Rocky Balboa" in the way of George Foreman coming back to win the heavyweight title from Michael Moorer 1994?

SS: No' not at all, where George coming back was something that he wanted to do for his church and his faith, Rocky is put in a situation where, his name is pulled up to compete in a charity event and there's all these little things that happen along the way that really just propels him forward to take on another obstacle in his life.

And you have to wonder, is ageism just another obstacle for Rocky to overcome in the latest movie, "Rocky Balboa"? Could Rocky then go on the same way that, a fighter like Bernard Hopkins has…at least in terms of movie sequels?

SS: Most definitely, I mean, we address that right up front, there's a couple of scenes where Rocky has been put up in a charity event and he does very, well and there's a boxing commission that kind of puts Rocky before a battery of tests and he does everything and he's physically okay to go on. But they try to deny him his god-given chance to compete and he's like, "Hey I did everything that you asked of me?" So we definitely do take that on as it relates to ageism and where people tend to think that because you're past fifty you need to step aside and just let the parade kind of pass you by, so there's the potential for Rocky to go and continue to do things as long as he wants to do them.

This may be true, but when you look at the other Rocky films, you have so many questions about the great characters, that Stallone created during the late 1970's and 1980's. Was Rocky as a person, based on Sly himself or other people and how does he feel Rocky will be like in the latest movie, "Rocky Balboa"?

SS: A little bit of all of those things, Rockys' a part of myself and he also is a part of people that I knew around me growing up. In this latest film, he's a little bit older and you know, definitely wiser and these events that happen in his life helps him to as he says in the latest movie, "clean things out of the basement".

Whenever you think of Rocky, most people can't help but remember the awesomely great bad guys like, Clubber Lang, Ivan Drago, etc. who are presented as an obstacle for Rocky to overcome? As a fight fan you're often times left wondering…how did he come up with such great opponents? Was Clubber Lang based on Sonny Liston? How does a fighter like Antonio Tarver stack up against the likes of, "Clubber Lang, or even Ivan Drago as a "bad guy" in the latest film, "Rocky Balboa"?

SS: "To a certain extent, they're each loosely based on boxing history… I wanted some great characters and opponents that Rocky could stack up against who were very you know, believable. In this latest Rocky, I got to spar with Antonio Tarver for some of our fight scenes and I can tell you that our fight scenes were very fast, moving and intense. When you see the fight scenes in this latest film, I think you'll actually be amazed at the intensity that takes place between me and Antonio."

Antonio Tarver the guy who knocked out Roy Jones! Getting ready to take on Rocky…in the words of Apollo Creed, "It sounds like a damn monster movie"! What was it like to spar with Antonio Tarver compared to Apollo Creed?

SS: "No comparison really, no, in the first film we watched many boxing films and I was very young and put up in a ring and I boxed with Carl…*as actors*. With Antonio, it was a lot different he fought as a fighter would and it was a different type of fighting all together, than what we did in the first movie."

It's been of course rumored for many years, that Sly got the opportunity to spar with some of his costars from Carl Weathers and Dolph Lundgren to established fighters' such as; Ernie Shavers and the great, Roberto Duran…what was that actually like you would have to wonder?

SS: "Sparring with Shavers and Duran was much different for me than actually fighting with Antonio in, "Rocky Balboa". Duran and especially Shavers, that was like incredible, firepower coming at you all the time. Antonio on the other hand, fights more scientifically than those two guys, he stands back kind of like a "fencer" would and I would have to push my way inside to press the action."

Sly has always been a big fight fan and can be seen ringside for some of the most important fights of the past twenty years…what would he think is the best fight that he ever saw at ringside and who was the greatest fighter he ever saw first hand?

SS: The best fight and fighter that I've been able to see and I've been very lucky to have seen a lot of them firsthand. I would say that the Ali/Shavers fight was the greatest fight that I've had the chance to see over the past twenty years. For pure stamina and energy and power punching, with Shavers lasting the full fifteen rounds…wow, it was like all action right up to the end.

After Rocky, who became America's adopted son, Sly would then go off and have the incredible success of the "Rambo" movies, a character who becomes an anti-war hero, by the end of the first film…one can't help but think, what made him create an antihero like that so soon after the Vietnam War and how does he feel that character is going to parlay into the latest "Rambo-4" coming out in 2007? I believe you have an Edgar Allan Poe piece set to come out next year…who would have thought that Rocky could write, as well as act?

SS: "We're going to going to Thailand in January to start the filming of "Rambo-4" it has yet to be titled completely and that'll be coming out late next year, I'm very excited to be able to go off and do that, John Rambo is a very real character. "First Blood" was the greatest action movie I had made *back then* and I'm looking to top that with the latest, "Rambo". After that, I'll be putting out a movie on the life of Edgar Allan Poe, I wrote it a long time ago, back in 1970 and he's a fascinating guy who's a misunderstood artist/genius and this will be kind of… my take on him."

After accomplishing so much within such a short amount of time…has success actually changed Rocky any from the down and out pug/artist that he was or is Stallone a much changed man after entering the world of Hollywood? Has success spoiled Sylvester Stallone?

SS: "No, not at all…I was very young when I did the first "Rocky" and over time you go through life and you go through some changes that makes you realize how precious life really is and how important it is to take some chances on yourself or in your career. I feel very blessed to be where I'm at now and to have lived the life that I have. I think that that's extremely evident in the latest film, "Rocky Balboa" as a person and as a character I think I've come to terms with my choices. So, you get a little older you feel the need to challenge yourself and that's what the latest movie, "Rocky Balboa" is all about…challenging your self because you can…no matter your age."

POST-FIGHT: WRAP-UP

Immediately after this interview was done, Sly came out with the latest "Rocky" on December 21st 2006, days after this interview made the cover of Boxing Digest magazine…I was very proud of that accomplishment and I still am. In case you were wondering how I was able to both interview Sly Stallone and type it up and then e-mail it in to my editor in less than an hour here' my secret (as a writer, I always recommend doing this if you're ever pressed for time) I pre wrote and then pre-typed all of my questions…so that when interview time came, all I'd have to type would be Sly's answers to my questions. Fifty percent of my typed-up interview was already done by then and it only took me all of forty-five minutes or so to type it up and then send it in to my editor…not easy…but, I knew it could be done.

WRAP-UP:

To this day, I can only thank "God" and my father, Rick Scurti sr. for even getting me into boxing, (I still believe in my heart of hearts, that he could have been middleweight champion in the 1970's beating Hagler and Leonard and everyone else, even though he doesn't believe it) and my friends and family...thank you, everyone and God Bless you, all...I've been very lucky to have been born into such a great family and with such great friends...God Bless, everyone.

Printed in the United Kingdom
by Lightning Source UK Ltd.
135783UK00002B/138/P